T · h · e

GOSPEL

a · n · d   t · h · e

AMERICAN

D · R · E · A · M

T·h·e

GOSPEL

a·n·d   t·h·e

AMERICAN
D·R·E·A·M

BRUCE L. SHELLEY

MULTNOMAH

Portland, Oregon 97266

Scripture quotations are from the New International Version, ©1973, 1978, 1984 by the International Bible Society. Used by permission of Zondervan Bible Publishers.

Edited by Rodney L. Morris
Cover design by Krieg Barrie

THE GOSPEL AND THE AMERICAN DREAM
© 1989 by Multnomah Press
Portland, Oregon 97266
Multnomah Press is a ministry of Multnomah School of the Bible, 8435 Northeast Glisan Street, Portland, Oregon 97220.

Printed in the United States of America

Library of Congress Cataloging-in- Publication Data

Shelley, Bruce L. (Bruce Leon), 1927-
    The Gospel and the American dream / Bruce L. Shelley.
        p.   cm.
    Includes bibliographical references.
    ISBN 0-88070-310-5
    1. Christianity—United States. 2. Christianity and culture. 3. United States—Church history—20th century. 4. United States—Moral conditions. I. Title.
BR526.S57   1989   89-37197
261'.0973—dc20   CIP

89 90 91 92 93 94 95 96 - 10 9 8 7 6 5 4 3 2 1

To our grandchildren,
Stacey, Zack, Kelsey, and Noel.
May they inherit the Gospel,
as well as a Dream.

Contents

Preface

It was, as I recall, the cartoon character Pogo who said, "The future ain't what it used to be." He was right.

After a life-changing experience in the U.S. Army, I entered the road to Christian ministry in the 1950s. It was still an honored profession in those days. My first parishioners in South Carolina called me "preacher Shelley," and the title was no put-down. I had access not only to Sunday singing conventions and grief-filled hospital rooms but to classrooms of public schools and platforms of civic events.

As the twenty-first century approaches, the future is here, and "it ain't what it used to be." In recent years televangelists have entertained the curious by disclosures of their sex scandals. Ministers all over the country have increased their insurance premiums as a hedge against potential lawsuits. And Roman Catholic prelates have faced angry picketers and media critics. Religion still makes the news, but the respect is gone.

In a largely secular public life, what place does religion fill in American culture? That question, it seems, assumes increasing importance for Christians, especially those men and women engaged in Christian ministry or soon to enter some church career. How can we communicate the gospel effectively if we are only vaguely aware of those forces shaping the lives of those to whom we speak?

As a church historian, one of my primary responsibilities is to interpret American culture for active,

and soon-to-be active, Christian ministers. In my introductory seminar within our Doctor of Ministry program, I have discovered in recent years that the
question of the gospel's encounter with American culture is more than a personal interest. Colleagues in
ministry assure me that my questions are theirs too.

I trace this background in order to make clear the
context and intent of this book. I am not presuming to
speak to specialists. I have in mind instead growing
numbers of American people who have not surrendered their minds to television and who are troubled
about the direction of American life. The book is
something of a social commentary from an evangelical
Christian who believes that a great many other Christians and Jews share a concern for America's future.
So the book is in part historical, in part pastoral,
which should be about what you might expect from a
church historian.

Much of what I have to say will seem obvious to
many people. That is not surprising since culture, like
the air we breathe, silently surrounds us and fills us.
As we all know, however, weather conditions change,
and we have to adapt to these shifting conditions.
What I am trying to provide, then, are a few observations on the wind currents and the ways our spiritual
lives are being affected by changing conditions.

I am persuaded that many American Christians,
and especially those in ministry, are befuddled by the
general impression they receive from the daily newspapers and other commentaries on American society.
"What is happening in this country?" they ask. "What,
in fact, is happening to my own people?" I am offering
here a somewhat tentative and introductory answer to
these questions.

Such questions among Christians are reflected in
the fact that hosts of white evangelical Protestants—perhaps more than thirty million of them—
have joined their black brothers and sisters in their
long-standing anger and discontent over conditions in
twentieth-century America. Millions of evangelical

Protestants, 20 percent of the electorate, have entered the political arena in recent years in the hopes of turning the country "back to God."

The most prominent example of this discontent, the so-called Christian Right, became in the 1980s a well-publicized part of the political scene. Baptist minister Jerry Falwell, followed by scores of lesser-known preachers, contended that America had rejected the advice of the Great Physician and showed definite signs of a deadly sickness. Many other evangelicals, less sure of what ails America and far less sure of the remedy, nevertheless share Pastor Falwell's concern. Their agreement with him lies in the meaning of the gospel and in America's spiritual need.

Since effective communication of the gospel depends upon some understanding of the people with whom we share the good news, we want to ask, in Part 1, who are these people called Americans? Can we identify "the American Dream"?

Americans, we will find, are individuals with certain characteristics that reflect their place in time and space. And American culture is a blend of at least four major strands or traditions.

The *biblical tradition* springs from the ideals of the Puritans, who brought to these shores a "myth of America" that was later adapted to the struggle for independence and nationhood. This struggle united the biblical and the *republican traditions* to form what we often think of as traditional America.

A significant transformation of American culture came, however, after the Civil War when the country was swept into the modern world through the forces of industry, commerce, and urbanization. In urban America other dreams gained prominence. Change, industry, progress became the incentives of the *economic tradition* in America. Then a bit later, after World War II, the economic tradition blended with the final strand of culture, the *therapeutic*, which promises personal healing and happiness through the securing of previously denied freedoms and rights.

Many white Protestant Christians feel uncomfortable in contemporary America because their dreams arose in traditional America. They react to the contemporary gospel of self because it seems to undercut religion, morality, commitment, and civic responsibility. They have become, in effect, exiles in their own homeland.

Christians who experience this cultural conflict encounter tensions in both their public and their private lives. So in Part 2 we turn to three ideals in American public life where Christians are often troubled: the place of religion in public life, the self-interest that dominates today's images of political freedom, and the "value-free" public education in America.

Then, in Part 3 we look at private life, where many Christians struggle with biblical standards and cultural influence. Four ideals in our private lives—success, work, family, and love—reflect the same tensions with contemporary American culture that we discover in public life. I am not suggesting in the least that these ideals are the only dreams Americans seek. We might have considered, for example, the place of sports or entertainment. I have simply chosen these seven public and private ideals as representative aspects of American culture that often appear in ministry to American people.

I suspect that my use of the name *Christian* in the book also requires some explanation. From time to time all Christian groups—Catholics, liberal Protestants, evangelicals, Orthodox, charismatics—tend to equate *Christian* with their own distinctive tradition. There are reasons for this practice, but they are not part of my intention here. I am using *Christian* in a basic and elementary sense of those common elements that have marked Christianity's place in American culture. If at times the usage seems to concentrate on the evangelical Protestant tradition, it is because this tradition, rooted in Puritanism, has played such a culturally significant role.

Finally, in Part 4, I want to suggest some possible directions for Christian responses to American life in the future. In this chapter, as well as all the earlier ones, I hope it is clear that I have no intention of forcing Christians to choose between being Christians and being Americans. We are both as long as we live in this country and confess that Jesus Christ is Lord. I am simply trying to make the reader aware of those ways in which the belief systems clash. In other words, what is distinctive about being a Christian in America?

The bibliography provides a long list of books that have shaped my thinking, including—I am eager to confess—those by Robert Bellah, Joshua Meyrowitz, A. James Reichley, Harry Blamires, Charles Colson, and Richard John Neuhaus. I am also grateful for two colleagues who took time to read these pages and offer me their reactions: my son Marshall, editor of *Leadership* journal, and Ralph Covell, my dean and fellow student of cross-cultural communication.

PART 1

LAND OF DREAMS

The ministry of the gospel is inextricably linked with understanding people. In this first part of our study we want to define our basic terms—gospel, culture, dream—and ask, Who are these people called Americans, and what do most of them mean by "the American Dream"?

American culture today, we find, is a blend of at least four major traditions. The biblical tradition, springing from the ideals of the Puritans, and the republican tradition, embodying our political institutions, came together in the nineteenth century to form traditional America. After the Civil War, however, the country was swept into the modern world, where other dreams gained prominence. Growth, industry, and commerce became the expressions of the economic tradition in America, and since World War II, the therapeutic tradition has promised Americans personal health and happiness through the gaining of previously denied freedoms.

In contemporary America, then, the gospel challenges the dreams of success and self-expression, which often leave little room for religion, morality, commitment, or public service.

Chapter One

America the Ugly?

"It is permissible, I think, for those of us who disapprove of the arrogance of the Moral Majority to borrow some of their memories."

—Neil Postman
in *The Disappearance of Childhood*

*I*n 1987 daily newspapers in the American West reported that Craig Corbett, the homosexual lover of the late Frank Batey, had won temporary custody of sixteen-year-old Brian Batey. Four years earlier Brian's Pentecostal mother had gained the support of fundamentalist Christians in Denver when she faced child-stealing charges for taking her son from his homosexual father. After a court battle for custody, a California judge at that time ruled in favor of Frank Batey.

So Brian lived for about three years with his father and his father's "lover" Craig Corbett. When Frank died of an AIDS-related illness early in 1987, Judge Judith McConnell awarded Brian's custody, not to his mother, but to his father's "lover."

When millions of Christians read the story in their morning papers, they asked, "What in the world is happening to this country?"

★ ★ ★

In 1983 the principal of the Harper Elementary School in Evansville, Indiana, told teacher's aide Mary May and several Christian coworkers that there would be no more Tuesday-morning meetings, or they would be fired!

What obscene or subversive thing had they done to provoke such an ominous warning? Drugs? Sexual abuse? Racial slur? Nothing of the sort. Since 1981 Mary May and her friends had been meeting before classes for prayer, Bible reading, and discussion. That was their crime! And it had to stop.

Mary May eventually sued the board of education and the superintendent of schools, claiming that the school board had violated her First Amendment rights to free speech, free association, and the free exercise of religion. She pointed out that other teachers and aides discussed politics, economics, and sports over their morning coffee before school. Why couldn't she and her friends talk about God?

A school-board representative explained that impressionable children might see "her carry a Bible to and from a meeting in their school, even if it is before classes. To children, teachers are strong authority figures." And, he added, school officials would be forced to make sure that no Bibles or other religious materials were left behind. "We don't want the children exposed to them."[1]

What in the world is happening to America?

★ ★ ★

For as long as people could remember, one of the highlights for Pawtucket, Rhode Island's predominantly Catholic citizenry was the annual Christmas display that included something for everyone: Santa Claus, Christmas trees, and the crèche scene with baby Jesus, Mary and Joseph, and assorted barn animals.

In the early 1980s, however, a few troubled souls challenged the presence of the crèche. It was paid for, it seems, by tax money. This made it, in their eyes, an infringement of the separation of church and state.

In 1984 the United States Supreme Court, in a 5-4 decision, upheld the city's right to display the crèche because, as Chief Justice Warren Burger expressed it, the crèche was merely "a neutral harbinger of the holiday season, useful for commercial purposes, but devoid of any inherent meaning." Is a faith "devoid of any inherent meaning" the only legally and culturally acceptable religion in contemporary America?[2]

What in the world *has* happened to America?

Every year, it seems, growing numbers of American Christians discover the fundamental conflict between the way of life as American society portrays it and the purpose of life as the gospel of the Lord Jesus Christ presents it. Almost daily we discover some new law, or new television show, or new public school policy that flies in the face of some Christian value.

American Christians find this public hostility to Christian symbols and practices hard to fathom. What about the pledge of allegiance to the flag? Doesn't that affirm that our nation is "under God"? Don't our coins still testify that we trust in God? Are we to believe that this is no longer a Christian country?

While many Christians would be hard-pressed to explain just how Christianity fits into traditional American life, they have an overpowering sense that things are not what they once were. The schools, the courts, the media—all seem determined to erase Christian influence from public life and confine religion to the four walls of the church or home. America the beautiful, in the minds of many Christians, is fast becoming America the ugly.[3]

In his *Fundamentalism and American Culture,* historian George Marsden describes how fundamentalists in the 1920s defended the traditional small-town American way of life even as the country was rushing to embrace the enlightened and liberated life-styles of urban America. Fundamentalists, says Marsden, were suddenly aliens in their own country. They didn't have to cross an ocean. They simply stood still while American culture changed around them.

During the last generation American culture has changed so much so fast that scarcely any Christian remains, conservative or liberal, Protestant or Catholic, who does not share the fundamentalist's sense of alienation. The dean of Harvard Divinity School, the Catholic Archbishop of Denver, and the editor of *Christianity Today* are all raising the same questions about Christianity and American public life.

Who can escape the questions about living as a Christian in a publicly secular America? If we view American culture as increasingly pagan—as we surely must do in the closing decade of the twentieth century—what changes can we expect the gospel to bring to American Christians and their churches? What does it mean for an American to genuinely repent? And when he begins to take seriously his confession, "Jesus is Lord!" what second thoughts does he have about his own, American, culture?

According to J. B. Phillips's translation of Romans 12:2, the apostle Paul urged Roman Christians, "Don't let the world around you squeeze you into its own mold." Apparently he knew the dangers of passive religion in a pagan society. Is the threat any less real in our own day?

To live and minister effectively in the United States at the dawn of the twenty-first century, Christians will need a clearer understanding of American culture and will have to probe the meaning of the gospel in new depths. Specifically, what are those forces in the American courts, schools, and media that try to squeeze us into their mold? What are those assumptions about reality in American culture that directly conflict with a Christian's life under the authority of Christ?

The most direct route to some understanding of American culture is that expression, often on the lips of politicians and in the appeals of commercials, "the American Dream."

The American Dream

The expression "the American Dream" is useful precisely because it can be twisted and shaped to one's personal tastes. To one person it is to make the Olympic team; to another it is to borrow $128,000 for her first home in suburbia; to a third it is to win the state's lottery. The clue to the Dream is in the dreamer.

Americans believe, above all else, in the dignity, indeed the sacredness, of the individual. We like to think of ourselves as and to raise our children to be self-reliant individuals. We try to find our true selves apart from any cultural or social influences. We feel supremely responsible to that self alone, and believe deeply that self-fulfillment holds the very meaning of life.

One of the first analysts of American individualism was the famous visitor and interpreter of American life in the 1830s, Alexis de Tocqueville. "Individualism," he wrote, "is a calm and considered feeling which disposes each citizen to isolate himself from the mass of his fellows and withdraw into the circle of family and friends; with this little society formed to his taste, he gladly leaves the greater society to look after itself."

Many people in a democratic society, said Tocqueville, "form the habit of thinking of themselves in isolation and imagine that their whole destiny is in their hands." Such people come to "forget their ancestors" and their descendants, as well as to isolate themselves from their contemporaries.[4]

The American Dream, then, is often a self-image of some future successful and admirable person who stands out from the crowd of ordinary people. For over a century now middle class Americans have imagined that the meaning of life lies in acquiring an ever-increasing status and income, and that personal happiness will come with the symbols of this success. The American Dream, then, usually stands for the image of someone who has "made it."

The American tradition has generated several models of this individualism, but in the last generation the dominant model has adopted a strikingly gaudy style. The bright shades of today's individualism reveal "the autonomous self," the self-seeking, pleasure-driven person, in Christopher Lasch's term, "the narcissist." Lasch writes:

> After the political turmoil of the sixties, Americans have retreated to purely personal preoccupations. Having no hope of improving their lives in any of the ways that matter, people have convinced themselves that what matters is psychic self-improvement: getting in touch with their feelings, eating health food, taking lessons in ballet or belly-dancing, immersing themselves in the wisdom of the East, jogging, learning how to "relate."[5]

Television advertisements in recent years reveal this preoccupation with self: One commercial for hair dye had a young woman say, "If I have only one life to live, let me live it as a blonde!" Another for a popular beer preached: "You only go around once in life, so grab for all the gusto you can." Another beer company ad dared to promise: "You can have it all!"

This recent version of the American Dream is obviously hostile to older ideas of moral order. It focuses not on the laws of God or any higher truths but on the autonomous individual who is supposedly able to choose the roles she will play in life and the commitments she will make. The standard for effectiveness in life is within the individual herself.

Individuals shut up in the solitude of their own hearts, striving desperately to get ahead of the pack, are not products of the gospel of the Lord Jesus Christ or the goal of Christian ministry in America.

The Bible teaches that God saw that it was not good for human beings to be alone, so he first created and then "recreated" persons for communion with himself, for fellowship in the common life of the church, and for the service of compassion in the world. This all begins when a person receives, personally and deeply, the Christian gospel. Unfortunately in American society today the meaning of the gospel is no longer self-evident. Perhaps, then, we ought to explain what we mean by it.

The Gospel

The gospel is essentially "good news." It is the story of an event of immense importance. When God decided to communicate with mankind, he sent his message wrapped in an Event: "God was reconciling the world to himself in Christ." So the gospel begins with Jesus Christ.

Jesus of Nazareth claimed divine authority. That is basic. This sense of divine mission was no strange psychological quirk. Hundreds of people who crossed Jesus' path recognized it. They found themselves confronted by a major decision. Would they join the scoffers who dismissed him as a troublesome dreamer, or would they follow him to God and be transformed?

One man, for example, a wealthy tax collector named Zacchaeus, invited Jesus to his home and found he had to reorder his whole lifestyle, beginning with the way he valued his money. When he expressed his willingness to change, Jesus said to him: "Today salvation has come to this house."

In recent years many Americans have tried to present Christianity as something charming and popular. They have painted Jesus as a religious teacher with unusual insight into human nature, but one without offense. That is absurd. Jesus Christ went about Galilee giving offense to all kinds of people. This young Jew was so inflammatory in his message that he was thrown out of synagogues, hounded from place to place, and finally arrested as a public nuisance.

Jesus' ministry reached a climax in his death, which secured for him his unique place in Christianity. Death came as no surprise. He expected the opposition of the Jewish authorities to lead to serious conflict. More than once he mentioned his approaching death to his disciples. He knew his claim to divine authority was not a popular one. At his trial the Jewish leaders told the Roman governor, "We have a law, and according to that law he must die, because he claimed to be the Son of God."[6]

When the crucifixion came, it struck his disciples as a tragic enigma. Death was a contradiction to the life of Jesus. He had been so often the victor. Why was he now so obviously death's victim?

The disciples discovered the answer to that question in the startling sequel to the crucifixion, Jesus' resurrection from the grave. After three days in the tomb, he returned to them. On several occasions he offered them evidence that death could not hold him. They saw then the significance of the cross. This extraordinary thing was nothing less than an act of God. Jesus died as a sacrifice for the sins of men and women, and was raised again to life by the power of God in order to provide forgiveness and spiritual power for all who believe in him.

A bit later, during the Jewish festival called Pentecost, the Holy Spirit descended upon the disciples and empowered them to witness boldly of the significance of Jesus' life, death, and resurrection. Peter dared to tell his Jewish kinsmen, "God has made this Jesus, whom you crucified, both Lord and Christ."[7]

That was the birth of the Christian gospel. The disciples believed, as Michael Green, the Anglican scholar, has put it, that within the confines of a human life "the Ultimate had become embodied, the Absolute had become contemporary." From that revelation arose the Christian community, the church, the spiritual home of those who turn from the love of self to the worship of God.

The gospel, then, in its original sense, is good news about something exciting that God has done. It is about a new spiritual power that has entered into life. The dynamic fact that "God was reconciling the world to himself in Christ" brings to people's lives a new reason to live and to make a difference in their world. "Christ's love compels us," the apostle wrote, "because we are convinced that one died for all, and therefore all died. And he died for all, that those who live should no longer live for themselves but for him who died for them and was raised again."[8]

In the Scriptures, then, the kingdom of God is nothing less than the sphere of salvation. *Salvation* in the Bible, however, means more than simply turning to God (a conversion). It also carries the idea of living to God (holiness). The gospel is an invitation to submit to the rule of God in all spheres of life, including public life. It brings a new moral authority to our lives. Applied to the moral crisis in America, this suggests that the Christian response is neither a program for a new society nor a withdrawal into an inner world of the spirit.

Today, as always, Christians serve as light in the world. They must insist, along with their Jewish neighbors, that social problems are often moral problems because human beings are bound by moral laws of God's making and societies must respect them. If a community is to be healthy, it must recognize the sanctity of life, marriage, and property. Leaders must administer justice impartiality. People must consider promises binding. The state must be the servant of the people, not their master. It must make virtue easier than vice and must punish crimes against its citizens.

Christians, of course, are not the only citizens in the United States who believe these things. There is an American tradition, as we shall see, that began with our Puritan fathers but has broadened to include Roman Catholics, Jews, and even some generally moral citizens. It is the tradition that is sometimes called "Judeo-Christian" but one that we will call in these pages "biblical."

This moral tradition in American culture does not provide Christians, or any other religious group, with a political agenda. The gospel advocates no specific political program. It is good news about a way of life for all generations. American Christians, therefore, are obligated to be conscientious citizens, but they have no revealed truth that will automatically tell them how to vote. That is part of what it means to be a Christian in American culture.

Culture

What do we mean by culture? It may be helpful to start with a biblical word more familiar to Christians— the *world*. When the apostles used the term *world*, they sometimes meant the created order, sometimes humanity, and sometimes social forces that were often in conflict with the gospel. The third use is close to what we might call *culture*.

In using *culture*, however, we have to exercise care, because we often think of culture in a rather narrow sense. We use the word in this way when we say, "She is a cultured person." We mean, of course, that she is educated and refined. She has good taste in music, food, and the arts.

In speaking of American culture, however, we have more than "high culture" in mind. In the study of peoples—often for missionary purposes—culture does not refer to upper-class people who get their pictures in the paper when they attend the symphony. Culture, as we are using the word, points to a person's life in the world, regardless of class. Attendance at the opera may be a true expression of their culture for some people, but screaming at a football game or betting at a cockfight are just as much a part of another people's way of life.

Culture is the pattern of meaning that a society uses to understand and evaluate itself. It helps to explain the beliefs and behavior within a society. Since culture develops, it has a history, so it frequently takes the form of tradition. Culture, then, designates a people's link with the past (their tradition) and their constant attempts to express themselves not only in abstract ideas but especially in their material creations.[9]

Language and customs are usually two of the most obvious expressions of culture. But the significant core of culture that often conflicts with the gospel is found in a people's search for the meaning of existence and the norms of acceptable behavior growing out of that understanding of reality. Scholars call this core of culture a people's "religion" or "myth."[10]

The problem of the gospel in American culture today is evident when we ask, What changes in the way of life does the gospel bring to an American? The conflict of the gospel with culture is easy to see today in a Muslim country. For example, when zealous Iranians in the 1970s thought that Christians in the Near East were a threat to their traditional way of life, they lashed out in anger and violence.

The same thing happened to Christians in the early church. In one of the earliest instances, orthodox Jews accused Stephen, the Christian evangelist, of teaching "that this Jesus of Nazareth will . . . change the customs Moses handed down to us." In a similar way, some merchants of Philippi charged the apostle Paul and his friend Silas with "throwing our city into an uproar by advocating customs unlawful for us Romans to accept or practice."[11]

In both cases, one Jewish and the other Roman, the issue focused on "customs," either the abandonment of old customs or introduction of new ones. When their customs were threatened, both Jews and Romans were deeply disturbed.

The gospel in America has reached a similar stage in our own time. In public schools, the media, and the courts, Christians are considered a threat to that strand of American culture that bases individual freedoms upon a therapeutic image of the American Dream.

Are we suggesting that Christians are always committed to the overthrow of existing culture? Not at all. The problem is more complex than that. Human culture can be in harmony with the gospel, it can be neutral, or it can be contrary to the rule of God.

The Lausanne Covenant, signed by nearly three thousand evangelicals at the Lausanne Congress on Evangelization in 1974, says, "Because man is God's creature, some of his culture is rich in beauty and goodness. Because man is fallen, all of it is tainted with sin and some of it is demonic. Culture, therefore, must always be tested and judged by Scripture."

If they are to "seek first the kingdom of God and his righteousness," American Christians will need the clear teachings of the Bible and the discernment of the Holy Spirit to decide what they can approve in American culture and what they must renounce. Believers who cut free entirely from their society usually find themselves rootless and insecure people. But Christians who never question their culture are usually shaped by public opinion rather than the love of Christ. That is the danger American Christians face as the twenty-first century approaches.

The sense of alienation from their own culture that Christians often feel is traceable to the fact that Christianity no longer shapes American culture like it once did. The United States has participated, along with Canada and Europe, in the historical trend called secularization. This is the process that removes Christian beliefs and symbols from more and more areas of public life. As a result, Christians today find it increasingly difficult to pursue "the American Dream" in the way their fathers did. The Dream itself has changed. As a result, Christians feel like aliens in their own country, exiles from the honor that once attended the term *Christian*.

How has the Dream changed? Consider just one example, representative of hundreds. In April 1987 the U.S. District Court in Washington D. C. ruled in the *Kendrick v. Bowen* case that federal funds must be denied any church-related organization that stresses sexual abstinence as a means of preventing pregnancy. Judge Charles Richey said that abstaining from sex before marriage was a "Christian value" and, therefore, could not be supported with federal funds. Fortunately, Judge Richey's decision was later overturned by the U. S. Supreme Court, but it is an example of how far the purge of Christian values has gone in America.[12]

For serious-minded Christians the consequences of this purge are rather obvious. We cannot accept the gospel of the Lord Jesus Christ without accepting simultaneously that transcendent realm of righteousness, the kingdom, over which he rules. It is precisely this kingdom or authority that prevailing American culture refuses to acknowledge. And this resistance to God's truth explains why the Christian must appear so often in America today as a rebel and a misfit.

The point is not that all benefits and symbols of America's earlier alliance with Christian values have now vanished. They have not. The point is that the direction of our cultural drift is away from the gospel and away from those truths about God and human nature and "the pursuit of happiness" that the gospel brings.

If things are what they seem, American culture is fast returning to a form of paganism. I can think of no better word for what is happening. Christians, therefore, must think clearly about the gospel and the American Dream, as well as dedicate themselves to the task of making clear to people in their often lonely and tragic search for personal happiness the special gifts that God promises to those who enter by faith into the fellowship of the gospel.

FURTHER READING

Charles Colson, *Kingdoms in Conflict* (1987)
Leslie Newbigin, *Foolishness to the Greeks* (1986)
Robert E. Webber, *The Secular Saint* (1979)

Chapter 1, Notes

1. Nat Hentoff, "Religion on School Property," *Washington Post*, 1 November 1984, sec. A.

2. *New York Times*, 6 March 1984.

3. Perhaps the best example of this shrill cry from conservative Christians is Jerry Falwell's *Listen, America!* While outlining the political agenda of the so-called Christian Right, it itemizes the moral offenses committed in recent American culture.

4. Quoted in Robert N. Bellah and his team's *Habits of the Heart* (New York: Harper & Row Publishers, 1985), 37.

5. Christopher Lasch, *The Culture of Narcissism* (New York: Warner Books, 1979), 29.

6. John 19:7.

7. Acts 2:36.

8. 2 Corinthians 5:14-15.

9. One of the widely used definitions of *culture* is "the sum total of ideas, conditioned emotional responses, and patterns of habitual behavior which members of [a given] society have acquired through instruction or imitation and which they share to a greater or less degree." Ralph Linton, *The Study of Man* (New York: Appleton-Century-Crofts, 1936), 288.

10. The use of *myth* does not suggest a fairy tale or lie. It means a way of looking at the world which helps to explain what the world is like and one's own place in it. It is close to our popular term *dream*.

11. Acts 6:14; 16:20-21.

12. *Focus on the Family*, August 1987, 4.

Chapter Two

This Is My Country?

"The American could always believe . . . that he could, if he wished, move on in space. He could ignore the traditional boundaries of habit, class, custom, and law and begin anew, unfettered by these ancient restraints."
— Sidney E. Mead
in *The Lively Experiment*

*T*oward the end of the eighteenth century, when the surging tides of war between the French and English for empire in America waned, men who had fought the battles were left behind. Among them was an articulate Frenchman named J. Hector St. John de Crèvecoeur. He settled on a farm in western New York and wrote of his adopted homeland. In his *Letters from an American Farmer* he asked the question that continues to trouble those who minister in the United States, "What then is the American, this new man?"

Crèvecoeur answered, "He is either an European or the descendant of an European . . . who leaving behind him all his ancient prejudices and manners, receives new ones from the new mode of life he has embraced, the new government he obeys, and the new rank he holds." To this day this "new man" in the new land is central to the understanding of American culture.

Most of us take our own culture for granted. That is the way culture works; we just assume that reality is pretty much the way we experience it. That makes it hard for us to explain to an outsider what our culture is like. "If you want a definition of water," says a Chinese proverb, "don't ask a fish."

Missionaries going to another culture, however, know the importance of understanding that culture. If they hope to explain the gospel in a meaningful way, they must not only know the good news about Jesus Christ, they must understand the culture of the people in their host country.

If American culture has changed as dramatically as it now appears, then the time has come for American Christians to view their homeland not as a Christian nation but as a mission field. Can we assume any longer that public life in the United States reflects Christian language, values, or morals? If not, then it is time to ask, What is an American? What sort of culture shapes his life? And how can we make the gospel intelligible to him?

But where do we begin to understand these people called Americans? We can do two things. We can take a look at American beginnings, and we can note those peculiar characteristics of American life that have impressed observant visitors to the United States.

America in Time and Space

Americans, like most other people, occupy a special place in time and space. Their niche in human history reveals their cultural roots. All their basic institutions—state, church, and family—go back primarily to Great Britain and, through Christian Europe, even further back to ancient Rome, Greece, and

Palestine. In a word, America is a western nation. Its values, customs, and institutions are products of a Christian past.

Specifically, the discovery of America was simultaneous with the birth of Protestantism. That fact alone explains a great deal about American culture. Martin Luther was nine years old when Christopher Columbus made his fateful voyage in 1492. Four decades later England renounced papal authority over the English people as Europe plunged into a century of religious wars between Catholic and Protestant. Zeal for Protestant supremacy in Great Britain was reflected in the fact that the Christian faith was responsible for the establishment of more colonies in America than any other single factor.

The Mayflower Compact of the Pilgrims captured the spirit, not only of their own church, but of many other colonists: "We . . . having undertaken, for the glory of God, and advancement of the Christian faith . . . a voyage to plant the first colony in the northern parts of Virginia, do . . . covenant and combine our selves together into a civil body politic."

Given the conditions in Europe, America soon became a religious mosaic of an assortment of Christian denominations. Most of them were English, Protestant, and Puritan, but the pluralism within this tradition made any long-range plans of a single state church in America an impossibility. Religious liberty seemed to be the country's destiny from the start.

The environment of the New World, however, proved at least as decisive in the formation of the American character as the time of its birth. The great spatial fact of American culture was the frontier. For almost three hundred years Americans lived in the continuing presence of the great West, the land of opportunity. Great empty spaces brought a passion for freedom to the American soul and body.[1]

In the century between 1787, when the United States became a nation, and 1890, when the frontier was officially closed, one of the most stupendous achievements of recorded human history transpired. In that brief century Americans tamed a continent stretching twenty-five hundred miles "from sea to shining sea." This extended experience on the frontier gave to Americans their sense of spaciousness, their lust for mobility, their reverence of independence, and their spirit of optimism.[2]

Can we identify, then, from our Protestant past and our frontier experience, those features of American culture that mark the unique ways the gospel enters into American life?

If we picture American culture as a great river system—let us say the Mississippi and all its tributaries—then we can imagine a large and shifting stream. American culture rushes on today, energized by currents from many sources: Latin Americans, for example, Southeast Asians, and voices from the New South. Many scholars, however, contend that it is still possible to identify a dominant culture in America, and it will be helpful for our purposes if we keep this main stream in mind.

The main current, it seems, fed by the various streams of American culture, is marked by a pervading individualism. Several scholars have suggested that America's mythic heroes provide insightful clues to the unique way Americans look at life and their own role in it.

A traditional American hero was the cowboy. In western lore he is nearly always the courageous individual who rides into a small town in the grip of some ruthless rancher or bloodthirsty gang. By his personal courage and special skill with a gun, he overthrows the bad guys and gains the admiration and gratitude of the community. But he almost never marries the schoolteacher and settles down. No, he rides off into the sunset alone, because the myth teaches that you can be a truly good person, worthy of admiration and love, only if you resist joining the community.

A more recent model of the courageous but lonely individual is the hard-boiled urban detective. He is seldom a success in conventional terms. Working out of his shabby office, he is wily, smart, and tough, but never fully appreciated. He always pursues justice and help for the unprotected even when it tears apart the fabric of society. In fact, the private eye, in defending the abused individual, nearly always discovers that society is corrupt to the core.

In these heroes, scholars tell us, we can discover the dominant trait of American culture: self-confident, down-to-earth individualism. "We insist . . . on finding our true selves independent of any cultural or social influence, being responsible to that self alone, and making its fulfillment the very meaning of our lives."[3]

When we say "American," then, what cultural traits of this pervasive individualism set us apart from other peoples? Over the years a number of foreign guests have visited the United States and recorded their impressions of American life. Drawing upon these observations, we can summarize at least six prominent American idiosyncrasies.

Prominent American Idiosyncrasies

1. Americans are optimistic. They care less about the past than about the future.

America's teen years were the nineteenth century, the Age of Progress. Throughout Europe and North America people looked to the future optimistically. For the American, however, progress was more than a dogma. It was an experience. Looking back over the century, historian Henry Steele Commager noted, "Nothing in all history had succeeded like America."[4]

In ten short decades Americans saw the New World wilderness converted to rich farmlands, villages transformed into cities, and the nation ascend to international wealth and power. Politicians came to speak of America's "manifest destiny" and "new frontier." Both nature and history, it seemed, justified the American's optimism. His experience taught him that, if he really wanted, he could change anything. Things that other peoples had only imagined became concrete realities in the American experiment.[5]

Unlike the European who lived so much in the past, the American lived for the future. He had little sense of the past or concern for it. He came to believe that nothing was beyond his power. The realities of geography and history constantly challenged his imagination, so he dreamed of expansive futures and projected ambitious plans.[6]

Henry Ford spoke for most Americans when he dismissed history as "bunk." Social radicalism seems to be in the American's blood. "What has existed in the past, especially the remote past, seems to him not only not authoritative, but irrelevant, inferior, and outworn. . . . But his enthusiasm for the future is profound. . . . It is the necessary faith of the pioneer."[7]

The American's dreams of a new day are nearly always marked by bigger and better material creations because the future he foresees is no distant utopia. It is rather some happy expansion of conditions he has already experienced. He dreams, says Spanish-born George Santayana, of number, measure, economy, and speed. "All his life he jumps into the train after it has started and jumps out before it has stopped; and he never once gets left behind, or breaks a leg. . . . Idealism in the American . . . goes hand in hand with present contentment and with foresight of what the future very likely will actually bring." In a word, the American "believes he is already on the right track and moving toward an excellent destiny."[8]

That helps to explain why Americans find it almost impossible to accept the dark side of the Christian message. They have no ear for the Christian "bad news" that precedes the "good news." The doctrines of original sin, Satan, and hell have all been taken with something less than seriousness in America. After all, how can Americans be damned? Evidence of God's favor surrounds them constantly. Jefferson spoke for most of them when he acknowledged an overruling Providence which proves by its "dispensations" that it delights in the happiness of man in the present life and greater happiness hereafter.[9]

2. Americans are mobile, a people open to constant change.

A century and a half ago, when Tocqueville took his studied look at America, he noted: "Every one is in motion." This mobility is more than physical; it is spiritual. Something better lies just ahead, because the American assumes she is endowed with a faculty for indefinite improvement.[10]

In more recent years another Frenchman, Catholic philosopher Jacques Maritain, noticed the same characteristic. "Americans" he wrote, "seem to live in their own land as pilgrims. . . . They are always on the move. . . . They are not settled, installed. . . . A skyscraper in New York does not lay claim to brave the centuries any more than does a tent in the desert."[11]

Even today international guests and immigrants continue to be struck by the fact that America is a nation on the go. It always has been. Perhaps it always will be. Today's summer campers are a fit symbol of the covered wagons of an earlier day. Census figures tell us that one of five Americans moves every year. That is 20 percent of our population!

Apparently, the frontier experience became a national habit. Westward-moving Americans had few local attachments, freely pulled up stakes for something better, and settled easily in new communities. In the twentieth century, when they constructed their secular cities, their mobility only intensified. Everything in the city shouted motion: the cloverleaf, the elevators and escalators, the airport control tower, the subways.

This incessant motion reflects the American's impatience with life. Maritain concluded that Americans "are not patient with their own life, as a rule. And they get disturbed and discouraged very soon, if the work they have undertaken is slow to succeed."[12]

Effective pastors, priests, and rabbis in America have to learn early how to minister to this passing parade. People simply do not stay put. If they do not transfer to another town, they move to another religion.

Missions experts know that people on the move are notoriously open to new ideas, so mobility in America has proved to be both a blessing and a curse for the spread of the gospel. As the frontier moved relentlessly west, hosts of pioneers welcomed the stabilizing and civilizing influence of the Christian message. But in the twentieth-century secular city, when increasing numbers of Americans have come to think of the gospel as "the old-time religion," it has suffered the fate of antiquated ideas and dated hairstyles. It is left behind in the rush for something new.

3. Americans believe in equality and are shaped by the pressures of public opinion.

The American's passion for equality, Tocqueville noted, creates in him a hunger to judge everything for himself. It "gives him, in all things, a taste for the tangible and the real, a contempt for tradition and for forms."[13]

Andrew Jackson's election in 1828 marked the triumph of the common man in the democratic West, and since that day America has consistently refused to turn back to aristocracy or nobility in any form. We call our presidents "Ike" or "Teddy" or "the Gipper," and no one thinks of confusing them with royalty.

This American Dream of equality is not primarily political. It is social, cultural, and psychological. Perhaps even economic. The poor in the United States take for granted their right to luxuries and privileges that are the prerogative of only the rich in other countries.

"Nowhere," Professor Commager notes, "did the sense of equality manifest itself more ostentatiously than in the American's manners." More flagrantly than anything else American manners, or lack of them, "advertised the American's satisfaction in a classless society." With no royal court and no upper class nobility to practice social formalities, Americans conducted themselves pretty much as their instincts dictated.[14]

And in America, instincts tend to conform to pressures from the crowd. Genius, excellence, elitism, nobility—these are un-American. After years of study and teaching at Harvard, Santayana noted that in America the bubbles must swim with the stream. What is best in American life is compulsory. "You must wave, you must cheer, you must push with the irresistible crowd; otherwise you will feel like a traitor, a soulless outcast, a deserted ship high and dry on the shore."[15]

These pressures of equalization, as Maritain found, extend even to the academic community, where truth is supposed to reign. "Many an American professor," he noticed, "seems to be anxious not to be more brilliant or more original than the average member of the teaching community. After all, is not genius always harmful to mutual tolerance and a good state of affairs in the community, and is not mediocrity of good standing preferable to any occasion for jealousy, strife, and rivalry?"[16]

It is easy to see, then, why Americans, once they understand it, have trouble with the Christian message. The God of the Bible is no democrat, and the gospel of Christ is no product of public opinion. Christian truth is never subject to an approving ballot. It is good news about what God has done in human history to everyone's surprise, Jews, Greeks, and Americans. It claims to be inside information, a "Word" from God. It lends no support to the American dogma of "equal access," so in recent years it strikes most Americans as exclusive and undemocratic. What genuine American will support that?

4. Americans are materialistic but they temper their prosperity with their generosity.

Americans evaluate almost everything by quantity. When they ask what a man is worth, they mean his material worth. The same trait is visible in the American passion for population statistics, production records, sales statistics, and church attendance. Every American simply knows that the majority rules and that big is better.

The American lives, therefore, for more. With the growth of the country the American, says Commager, grew "accustomed to prosperity, resented anything that interfered with it, and regarded any prolonged lapse from it as an outrage against nature. The worst misfortune that could befall a political party was a depression, and the worst that could be said against a law was that it was harmful to business. Whatever promised to increase wealth was automatically regarded as good." As a result the American was tolerant of speculation, advertising, exploitation of the environment, and the ugly scars of industrialism. Something can be said for the impression that Americans worship the Almighty Dollar.[17]

Fortunately, what Tocqueville called this "tenacious, exclusive, universal passion" for prosperity has its limits.[18] One of the more obvious boundaries provided for American greed is a strong sense of humanitarianism. "What is serving God?" Benjamin Franklin once asked. " 'Tis doing good to man." There is no lack of evidence that Americans care for the less fortunate. It is obvious in our host of voluntary organizations, our tax laws, and our protection of minorities.

This humanitarianism not only restrains our materialism, it also forms a type of national religion. Many Americans view religion less by theology and authority and more by a faith in the American future and in the nation's resources for life in this world. This gospel of humanitarianism has sent Americans throughout the world distributing funds for foreign aid, commissioning groups such as the Peace Corps, and dying for the democratic system.[19]

It should not surprise American Christians, then, when their non-Christian neighbors care less about the beauty of their sanctuaries and more about their eagerness to feed the hungry, clothe the homeless, and sponsor the refugee. To most Americans, true religion is to lift up the fallen.

5. *Americans are activists; they are instinctively responsive to secularity.*

Will Herberg, the Jewish sociologist, once said, "America seems to be at once the most religious and the most secular of all nations." His apparently contradictory statement points to an American trait we might call *activism*.[20]

To most foreign guests, Americans appear to be forever rushing. There is a reason for it. The American frontier knew few conveniences, so Americans, drawing upon their Protestant ethic, developed a do-it-yourself spirit. "Get the job done" became an American slogan and the "can-do" spirit a national virtue.

Even our speech betrays our impatience. International students and refugees find our "Americanese" difficult because so many of our words are slurred and our sentences clipped. The same characteristic is evident in the way Americans think. While most Christian denominations in the United States are committed by their creeds to the doctrine that man is evil by nature, most Americans are unlikely to give the concept much thought. They much prefer to stress man's ability to change, to improve his condition.

This trait helps to explain the deep strain of activism in American religion. Saintliness has never been a conspicuous quality in the nation's religious leaders, and the American believer tends to resist the doctrine of salvation by grace in favor of an instinctive faith in salvation by works. The Social Gospel, we might recall, was an American movement.[21]

Nor was the all-this-and-heaven-too philosophy limited to religious liberals. Even in his time, before the rise of liberalism, Tocqueville observed, "The American ministers of the Gospel do not attempt to draw or fix all the thoughts of man upon the life to come; they are willing to surrender a portion of his heart to the cares of the present." While these ministers, he wrote, "never cease to point to the other world as part of the great object of the hopes and fears of the believer, they do not forbid him honestly to court prosperity in this [world]." Recent versions of this characteristic are obvious in the "health and wealth" and the "positive thinking" gospels.[22]

6. Americans are practical; they do not easily accept the supernatural.

Americans are supremely practical about nearly everything—politics, religion, culture, science. Theories and speculations disturb them. That is why theology and philosophy have never been big in America. Perhaps the nearest thing to an American philosophy is pragmatism, not because Americans are convinced it is true but because it comes close to what they call "common sense."

Even when Americans welcome the mythic religions of the East, such as the transcendental meditation and New Age crazes in recent years, they tend to turn religion into some technique for inward peace or stress management.

Tocqueville noticed this feature of American life in the 1830s. He wrote that "the philosophical method" of Americans consisted of as little philosophy as possible. The principal characteristics of their view of life was "to evade the bondage of system and habit . . . to accept tradition only as a means of information," and "to seek the reason of things for one's self, and in one's self alone."

Americans, he said, think that they can resolve, without outside assistance, all the little difficulties their practical life presents them. They readily conclude that everything in the world can be explained and that "nothing transcends the limits of their understanding." So they deny what they cannot comprehend. This leaves them "little faith for whatever is extraordinary, and an almost insurmountable distaste for whatever is supernatural." The significance for preachers of the gospel is obvious.[23]

What then do we mean by an American? We know there are immense differences between individuals, but we also recognize that Americans who share the nation's prevailing culture share a common environment, hosts of customs, a common temper, and many of the same thoughts. A single designation called "the American" can cover a large part of what each American is in his character and his religious outlook.[24]

FURTHER READING

Henry Steele Commager, *The American Mind* (1950)
Sidney E. Mead, *The Lively Experiment* (1963)
Edward C. Stewart, *American Cultural Patterns: A Cross-Cultural Perspective* (1972)
Alexis de Tocqueville, *Democracy in America*, ed. J. P. Mayer (1969)

Chapter 2, Notes
1. George Santayana, *Character and Opinion in the United States* (New York: W. W. Norton Co., 1967), 173.
2. See Henry Steele Commager, *The American Mind* (New Haven, Conn.: Yale University Press, 1950), 4-5.
3. See Robert N. Bellah and others, *Habits of the Heart* (New York: Harper & Row Publishers, 1985), 150.
4. Commager, *American Mind*, 5.
5. Anthony T. Padovano, *American Culture and the Quest for Christ* (New York: Sheed & Ward, 1970), 98.
6. Commager, *American Mind*, 5. In his *The American Adam* (University of Chicago Press, 1955), R. W. B. Lewis traces this future orientation in nineteenth-century literature. Novels and poems "described the world as starting up again under fresh initiative, in a divinely granted second chance for the human race, after the first chance had been so disastrously fumbled in the darkening Old World. . . . The new habits to be engendered on the new American scene were suggested by the image of a radically new personality, the hero of the new adventure: an individual emancipated from history, happily bereft of ancestry, untouched and undefiled by the usual inheritances of family and race; an individual standing alone, self-reliant and self-propelling, ready to confront whatever awaited him with the aid of his own unique and inherent

44 Land of Dreams

resources." In a Bible-reading generation that new hero was most easily identified with Adam before the fall (p. 5).

7. Santayana, *Character and Opinion*, 169.

8. Ibid., 174-76.

9. See Commager, *American Mind*, 164.

10. Alexis de Tocqueville, *Democracy in America*, trans. George Lawrence, ed. J. P. Mayer (New York: Doubleday, Anchor Books, 1969), 164, 157-58.

11. Jacques Maritain, *Reflections on America* (New York: Charles Scribner's Sons, 1958), 54-55.

12. Ibid., 27.

13. Tocqueville, *Democracy in America*, 163.

14. Commager, *American Mind*, 14-15.

15. Santayana, *Character and Opinion*, 210-12.

16. Maritain, *Reflections on America*, 43.

17. Commager, *American Mind*, 7. In 1854, after a decade in the United States, Phillip Schaff, the church historian, returned to Germany to give two lectures to his colleagues about *America*. "Whether the enormous increases of luxury, and worldly pomp, and splendor," he said, "will gradually undermine the Republic, whose proper foundation is the patriarchal style of simplicity and honesty, time will tell. At any rate the flourishing commerce and growing wealth of the country involves danger of a bottomless materialism and worldliness." He found in Christianity alone the powerful corrective to gain "predominance" over the "almighty dollar." See Philip Schaff, *America*, ed. Perry Miller (Cambridge, Mass.: Belknap Press of Harvard University, 1961), 52-53.

18. Quoted in *Democracy in America*, 212.

19. See Padovano, *American Culture*, 110.

20. Will Herberg, *Protestant, Catholic, Jew* (Garden City, N.Y.: Doubleday, 1955), 3.

21. See Commager, *American Mind*, 9.

22. Tocqueville, *Democracy in America*, 155.

23. Ibid., 143-44.

24. See Santayana, *Character and Opinion*, 168.

Chapter Three
Dreams in the Making

"We shall find that the God of Israel is among us when he shall make us a praise and glory that men shall say of succeeding plantations: 'The Lord make it like that of New England.' For we must consider that we shall be a city upon a hill."

—John Winthrop,
on board the *Arbella*, 1630

F or the American Christian perhaps the most impressive site among the many in the Washington D. C. area is the Lincoln Memorial, housing the massive statue of President Abraham Lincoln seated and looking out over an uncertain nation. It has served as the backdrop for hundreds of civic celebrations and public protests.

Within the memorial are inscribed two documents. On one side of the president is his Gettysburg Address; on the other is his Second Inaugural Address. Any tourist today can pause to read the message Lincoln gave to mark his second term in office. And any Christian is sure to be moved by Lincoln's struggle to find special meaning in the bloody conflict that so deeply divided the nation in his time:

> On the occasion corresponding to this four years ago, all thoughts were anxiously directed to an impending civil war. . . . Neither party expected for the war the magnitude or the duration which it has already attained. . . . Both read the same Bible, and pray to the same God; and each invokes his aid against the other. . . . The prayers of both could not be answered—that of neither has been answered fully.
>
> The Almighty has his own purposes. . . . Fondly do we hope—fervently do we pray—that this mighty scourge of war may speedily pass away. Yet, if God wills that it continue until . . . every drop of blood drawn with the lash shall be paid by another drawn with the sword, as was said three thousand years ago, so still it must be said, "The judgments of the Lord are true and righteous altogether."

Today, eloquence of that sort in the public square is conspicuous by its absence. Only a minority of Americans would recognize the biblical allusions and, more importantly, many Americans would resent a speaker's dragging "the Almighty" into an obviously secular event like the inauguration of a president.

Such a secular attitude helps to explain why many Christians today feel like aliens in their own country. They know very well that Lincoln was not alone in searching for the hand of the Almighty in the nation's conflict. The Christian gospel had so permeated American culture during the first two centuries of her history that most Americans at the time of the Civil War thought of their nation as part of a divine plan.

American courts, schools, and newspapers all regarded Christian beliefs and Christian behavior as central to the American way of life. While nearly

everyone happily accepted the separation of the institutions of church and state, practically no one imagined American public life stripped of the Christian
religion. Even through the bloody Civil War, God's
hand was upon America for a special purpose. Some
sense of "manifest destiny" was part of what it meant
to be an American.

Today, of course, all that has changed. Voices in
the courts, schools, and media offer us constant
reminders that religion is strictly private. Keep it out
of public life, they say. That is the American way.

Somewhere, somehow, visions of the American
Dream began to change. That much is obvious. Conservative Christians in particular believe the country
at some point in the past took a dangerous turn away
from the path of greatness and needs to recover its
sense of moral and spiritual direction. But where was
that deadly turn, and how did it happen?

Perhaps the best way to find that turn in the road
is to take a look at a contemporary map. It is obvious
today that Americans are traveling in several directions in pursuit of the American Dream. There is no
universally accepted highway to happiness. If we think
of cultural traditions as interstate routes through life,
contemporary American culture reveals that most
Americans are directed by four primary highways: the
biblical, republican, economic, and therapeutic routes.[1]

By examining such a map in this and the following chapter, we can trace the gospel's place in
American culture and discover that significant turn in
the road that led away from traditional, small-town
America, where biblical values so clearly shaped public life, toward secular-minded, urban America, where
the Christian witness is a faint echo in the din of
screaming commercials.[2]

The Biblical Tradition

The American sense of destiny reflected in
Lincoln's speech can be traced to our colonial Puritan

fathers. The Puritan's zeal to purify the Church of England was fired by the eager reading of popular versions of the Bible and by a view of history found in another widely read book, John Foxe's *Book of Martyrs*. Foxe marshaled account after account of the suffering of faithful Protestants who had dared to die for the triumph of God's kingdom. According to Foxe, the trail of martyrs led to the shores of England, to the reign of Catholic "Bloody" Mary, and to the courageous resistance of Protestant believers. His conclusion was clear: God had a special place for the English people in his worldwide plan of redemption.

Consequently, the Puritans who crossed the Atlantic came to think of themselves as God's new Israel, sent by the Almighty on a special mission into the American wilderness. Governor John Winthrop expressed this vision in his famous sermon aboard the *Arbella*: "We shall find that the God of Israel is among us when he shall make us a praise and glory . . . a city upon a hill." And what was that glory? It was to create out of the American wilderness a "holy commonwealth," a biblical society in which the will of God would be done in the state as well as in the church.

Before disembarking on American shores by the thousands, the Puritans entered a covenant which committed each person to an exemplary life. Moved by an intense moral zeal for the regulation of everyday conduct, the Puritans founded their community on this covenant which bound each individual to all the others, so that one's own sins imperiled not just oneself but the group. By failing to observe the demands of the covenant, a person could bring down God's wrath on the whole community.

The Puritans, then, planted in America a dream of a certain kind of ethical community. Principles for such a society derive from the Bible, and moral freedom is liberty, not to do whatever one wants, but to do the good, just, and honest thing. Many people in America today would like to forget that the Puritans ever came to the New World. The mere mention of their name is sufficient to arouse outbursts of emotion decrying religion in politics or denouncing some supposed censorship of school textbooks. In our Age of Self, no group seems more un-American than the founders of the New England colonies.

These critics, however, reveal more of their own passion for self-expression than they do any knowledge of American character. We may curse our great-grandparents but our opinions will never alter our genetic character. The Puritan story is written indelibly across the pages of the American saga.

John Winthrop, Cotton Mather, Jonathan Edwards, and all their train forged nothing less than the framework for our American identity. Two centuries after the Great Migration of Puritans to New England shores, Tocqueville wrote: "Democracy more perfect than any of which antiquity had dared to dream sprang full-grown and fully armed from the midst of the old feudal society. . . . [In this sense,] the whole destiny of America [is] contained in the first Puritan who landed on these shores, as that of the whole human race in the first man."

Contemporary Puritan scholar Sacvan Bercovitch has masterfully documented Tocqueville's observation. He argues that the Puritans established nothing less than the central tenets of what was to become our dominant culture. Since there was no competing order, the Puritan view of life reached to virtually all levels of American thought and behavior. The web of significance spun out by successive generations of Americans justified their way of life to themselves and to the world at large. It constitutes the major thread of American culture called "the American mission."

Thanks to the Puritans, nationalism in the United States has carried with it the Christian meaning of the sacred. Only in the United States has the national designation—America—united "nationality and universality, civic and spiritual selfhood, secular and redemptive history, the country's past and paradise to be, in a single synthetic ideal."[3]

True, the original form of the holy commonwealth did not endure. As early as 1670, aspiring merchants and landholders challenged the clerical control in the colony. Within two generations the religious foundations of the holy commonwealth began to crumble. Too many New Englanders made no profession of participation in the "covenant of grace" and were therefore unqualified for leadership in the biblical commonwealth.

The dream of the sacred mission in America, however, endured. Concern for an inward, life-changing experience of the grace of God was revived in the generation before the Revolutionary War in America's first spiritual awakening. The revival appeared first in the 1720s as a series of regional awakenings. But under the incendiary preaching ministry of John Wesley's friend, George Whitefield, the regional revivals merged into a Great Awakening that continued to burn until the American Revolution.

The revivalists of the Great Awakening no longer dreamed of creating a holy commonwealth as their fathers did. But by calling for an invisible transformation of the soul, they hoped to shape public thinking and to create by voluntary means "a nation under God." They still believed, as their fathers had, "Blessed is the nation whose God is the Lord."

In western Massachusetts Jonathan Edwards was convinced that the outpouring of the Spirit of God upon America was evidence that America would soon become the center of Christ's millennial kingdom. Most of the revivalists were so persuaded that God had visited America in the revival that they came to share the ideals of the colonial patriots and to lend their support to the War of Independence. This modification of the Puritan vision was unusually significant. The original Puritans held that they were God's chosen people because they had been given the one pure religion, English Protestantism. By the time of the American Revolution, the revivalists held that the American people were elect because of the civil liberty they defended against the anti-Christian tyranny of the British.

The Republican Tradition

This love of liberty, more than any other single factor, brought the biblical strand of American culture into an alliance with the republican strand. Revivalists cooperated with rationalists, the less-than-orthodox founders of the American republic, and provided much of the grass-roots energy for the American Revolution and the creation of a new nation.

A number of the influential Founding Fathers drank deeply from the wells of the eighteenth-century Enlightenment. The spirit of the Enlightenment in America was in part religious, but it was a religion inspired by a human-centered moral philosophy more than by the Christian revelation. These Fathers, led by Thomas Jefferson, the Adamses, James Madison and others, were convinced that a common moral philosophy rooted in human reason could provide a foundation for public life in America.

Delaware lawyer Caesar Rodney, in a letter to Jefferson, reflected the spirit of the Enlightenment:

> Every door is now open to the Sons of Genius and Science to inquire after Truth. Hence we may expect the darkening clouds of error will vanish fast before the light of reason; and that the period is fast arriving when the Truth will enlighten the whole world.

In simplified terms, republicanism was the conviction that power defined the political process and that unchecked power led to corruption, just as corruption fostered unchecked power. Thus, genuine republicanism tended to favor separation of power in government rather than its concentration. Governments must function for the common good (the "common weal" or the "commonwealth") instead of for the promotion of private privilege or the advantage of special leaders.

We may take Jefferson, the author of the Declaration of Independence, as representative of this republican strand in American culture. Though only thirty-three years of age when he drafted the Declaration, Jefferson spoke for a new people when he wrote "all men are created equal."

By equality he did not mean equal in all respects. He meant political equality, equal before the law. And he knew that this principle, while true at all times, can only function effectively in a republic where the citizens participate responsibly in government.

Jefferson held that the God who bestowed these rights was the benevolent Creator who preserves people in this life and judges them according to their moral worth. The question of God's existence, however, was secondary to Jefferson's concern for those "incitements to virtue" that could contribute to the good of society. People could be servants of society because all had been granted a common moral sense, a conscience to guide them to know the good and to do it.

Jefferson and the other enlightened republicans "drew a close connection between the morals of a people and the safety of its government—virtue in the public made it more likely that government would flourish, vice more likely that it would verge toward tyranny."[4]

Religion, however, posed special problems. Jefferson and his enlightened colleagues knew how disruptive religion could be to a successful political coalition. So they moved toward a constitutional arrangement granting religious liberty to all, not because religion was unimportant to the colonists but because it was too important to trust to a national establishment. That is why the Constitution speaks of religion in secular terms. Freedom of religion in the First Amendment ensured the American people that the national government would have no power to force a single religious position on them. The revivalists welcomed that arrangement because they saw ever more clearly the hand of God upon the new

nation. Many Christians argued, as the Congregation-
alist John Mullen did in 1797, "that the expansion of
republican forms of government will accompany that
spreading of the gospel . . . which the scripture
prophecies represent as constituting the glory of the
latter days."[5]

Thus, we have the peculiar church-state tradition
in America, which embraces two basic conflicting ideals.
One we might call the *custodial ideal*, rooted in the
Puritan vision of America. This view assumes that
society is organic and that civil authorities have a
responsibility for the spiritual as well as the physical
well-being of the nation. The other view we might call
the *plural ideal*. This holds that a critical difference
exists between public interests and private concerns.
Government is public; religion is private. The health of
both is aided by their strict separation.[6]

The custodial ideal was carried throughout the
young nation in the nineteenth century by the waves
of evangelical revivals. On the graph of the history of
Christianity in America, the curve of gospel influence
on American culture turns upward with the outbreak
of the Great Awakening in the 1720s. Then, after a lull
during the War of Independence, the curve surges for
new heights in the new-found freedom of the frontier,
until it reaches a peak in Lincoln's day.

Traditional America

In 1835, a generation before the Civil War, the
well-known New England minister Lyman Beecher
preached one of his more popular sermons. He called
it "A Plea for the West." The oration reveals Beecher's
deep-seated belief that a vast new empire was opening
in the American wilderness. Nothing less than a whole
culture was at stake. Christians should seize the opportunity, he said, and shape "the religious and political
destiny of the nation."

And how did Beecher propose to do all that? He
called for the preaching of the gospel, distribution of

Bibles, the planting of churches, the establishing of schools, and the reform of American morals.

This vision of a Christian America dominated evangelical thinking and generated what historians have called the "Righteous Empire." Before this empire began to fade from public view toward the end of the nineteenth century, it left its mark on the thinking of many Christians who drew their vision of America in large measure from the Bible.

As evangelicals faced the challenge of winning a nation to Christian obedience, two instruments were available to them: revivals and voluntary societies.

America's first Great Awakening created an evangelical fixation upon revivals as God's special instrument for reforming the American people. As the nation spread westward, spiritual awakenings occurred in the newly settled regions between the Alleghenies and the Mississippi and proved to be a primary channel for the spread of Christianity and the civilizing of the wilderness.

Since the then-recently adopted American Constitution and Bill of Rights rejected any thoughts of a "holy commonwealth" by ruling out any direct influence of the churches upon the government, how were these growing numbers of Christians to fulfill their responsibilities for public life and morals? That is where the voluntary societies came in. William Carey and other English evangelicals had designed the voluntary society to carry the gospel to India and to fight the slave trade in the West Indies. The societies allowed individual Christians, without regard to denominational identities, to mobilize their efforts for moral or religious causes. They simply contributed their money, and in some cases their lives, to advance their cause at home or overseas. A board of directors, often laymen, oversaw the work of the society, much as a board of directors supervised the business of a trading company.

American evangelicals seized the idea for their own purposes. It seemed the perfect instrument for America's free society. Thus early in the nineteenth century scores of societies sprang up to shape some aspect of American life: Bible societies, sabbath societies, mission societies, temperance societies. "One thing is becoming daily more evident," said Beecher in 1830, "the grand influence" of the church and the triumphs of the last forty years are the result of the "voluntary association of Christians."

That grand influence of the churches included the shaping of American morality and many commonly shared religious beliefs. In camp meetings and revivals all across America, through educators such as President Timothy Dwight of Yale and circuit-riding preachers such as Peter Cartwright, in ten thousand classrooms where a million *McGuffey Readers* were opened for the daily reading lesson, evangelical Christianity emerged as the dominant faith in America before the Civil War.

James Bryce's tribute published in 1894 was especially true of the generation just before the Civil War. "No political party," he wrote, "no class in the community, has any hostility either to Christianity or to any particular Christian body. The churches are as thoroughly popular, in the best sense of the word, as any of the other institutions of the country."[7]

But how did this evangelical vision of a biblical society shape American life?

In the nineteenth century local churches in America's small towns were the heart and soul of Protestant Christianity. When Tocqueville visited the country in the 1830s, he expressed his admiration for the democratic process at work in the numerous small communities throughout the nation.

He held that American democracy was always in danger of disintegrating into a selfish pack of mutually antagonistic individuals. But he found a bulwark against such a mass society in America's small towns, where most people were self-employed, civic-minded, and influenced, directly or indirectly, by the Christian faith.

This vision of a democratic America, linking

Christian values and republican principles, was probably the prevailing vision throughout the nineteenth century. Few dared to stand and challenge President Woodrow Wilson when he said, "America was born a Christian nation for the purpose of exemplifying to the nations of the world the principles of righteousness found in the Word of God."[8]

To this day, if we try, we can still hear confident voices across America singing,

> O beautiful for pilgrim feet,
> Whose stern impassioned stress
> A thoroughfare for freedom beat
> Across the wilderness!
> America! America! God mend thine ev'ry flaw,
> Confirm thy soul in self-control,
> Thy liberty in law.

This prevalence of the gospel in America's past, then, explains the Lincoln Memorial in Washington. Now we know why, when the slavery crisis plunged the nation into its bloodiest conflict, interpreters of the war, including President Lincoln himself, turned to the biblical themes of judgment, suffering, and atonement to explain the nation's tragedy. This bit of history also explains why so many Christians today, as ready as any other American to wave the flag and pledge allegiance to "one nation under God," feel at times like a thankful but misunderstood minority.

FURTHER READING

Robert N. Bellah and others, *Habits of the Heart* (1985)

Sacvan Bercovitch, *The American Jeremiad* (1978)

John F. Wilson and Donald L. Drakeman, eds., *Church and State in American History* (1987)

John D. Woodbridge, Mark A. Noll, and Nathan O. Hatch, *The Gospel in America* (1979)

Chapter 3, Notes

1. I am using *tradition* here in the sense that Robert Bellah and others use the term, as a "pattern of understandings and evaluations that a community has worked out over time." Tradition in this sense is an ongoing reasoned argument about the good of the community or institution whose identity it defines. See Robert N. Bellah and others, *Habits of the Heart* (New York: Harper & Row, 1985), 335-36, and Alasdair MacIntyre, *After Virtue: A Study in Moral Theory* (Notre Dame, Ind.: University of Notre Dame Press, 1981), 206-7. Bellah and his associates call these four cultural traditions biblical, republican, utilitarian, and expressive individualism. Two decades earlier Philip Rieff also found four models for the conduct of life but calls them religious, political, economic, and psychological. See his *The Triumph of the Therapeutic* (New York: Harper & Row, 1966), 58.

2. While accepting Bellah's argument that the four strands of American culture have existed since the birth of the nation, we will follow Mark Noll's lead in his *One Nation Under God? Christian Faith and Political Action in America* (San Francisco: Harper & Row, 1988) when he notes that it is possible to differentiate three quite distinct periods in American history. The colonial period under the influence of the *Puritans*, the national period under a more general *evangelical* influence, and a modern period under the sway of the *secular* (p. 22). We will refine this slightly by distinguishing the period after the Civil War, when *big business* dominated American culture and the period after World War II, when *therapy* achieved pervasive influence.

The important term is *hegemony*. Sacvan Bercovitch uses it to designate "historically organic" ideology, based on cultural leadership and "spontaneous consent," as distinct from ideologies imposed by "state coercive power." See Bercovitch, *The American Jeremiad* (Madison, Wis.: University of Wisconsin Press, 1978), xiii.

3. Bercovitch, *American Jeremiad*, 19, 9, 176. Bercovitch refers to the Puritan vision as a "myth." By "myth" he does not mean a fairy tale or lie. He means a way of looking at the world which helps explain that world and one's place in it. The "myth" tells us what is important and meaningful out of all of life's options.

Bercovitch traces the spread of this myth through the first three centuries of American history by studying the use of the *jeremiad*, the political sermon, "what might be called the state-of-the-covenant address," delivered at public occasions such as days of fasting, thanksgiving, covenant renewal, and elections.

These sermons or addresses nearly always spoke to some social disobedience, some betrayal of the covenant, the degeneracy of the youth, the lure of profits and pleasures, and to the danger of God's swift punishment. Since the colonists, however, were God's chosen people, this punishment was not aimed at their destruction, but at their correction. "The purpose of the jeremiad was to direct an imperiled people of God toward the fulfillment of their destiny, to guide them individually toward salvation, and collectively toward the American city of God" (p. 9).

4. Noll, *One Nation Under God?*, 38. See also George Marsden's survey of religion and American politics in "Politics and Religion in American History," *The Reformed Journal*, October 1988, 11-16.

5. See Nathan O. Hatch, *The Sacred Cause of Liberty* (New Haven, Conn.: Yale University Press, 1977), 139.

6. These two labels for the contrasting positions are from Grant Wacker's "Uneasy in Zion: Evangelicals in Postmodern Society," in *Evangelicalism and Modern America*, ed. George Marsden (Grand Rapids: Wm. B. Eerdmans Publishing Co., 1984).

7. James Bryce, *The American Commonwealth*, 3d ed. (New York: Macmillan, 1908), 2:711.

8. Quoted in Martin E. Marty, *Righteous Empire* (New York: Dial Press, 1970), preceding Contents page.

Chapter Four

Nightmares in the Secular City

"I can remember . . . when the first automobile rolled down main street of my native village. . . . And I remember when the first motion picture invaded the town. No one took them seriously at first. . . . But everyone knows by this time that these instruments have changed not only how we express ourselves but what we believe and do."
—Herbert Wallace Schneider
Religion in Twentieth-Century America (1952)

During the summer of 1925 the lawn of the courthouse square in Dayton, Tennessee, was crowded with country folks, women in their print dresses and men in their shirt sleeves and galluses. They were there, like the radio men from WGN Chicago, to follow the unfolding trial of John Scopes within the red brick courthouse. No other event in the 1920s so clearly depicts the winds of change sweeping over America.

The issue before the court in the highly publicized trial was whether John Scopes, the young high school biology teacher, had violated a recent Tennessee law prohibiting the teaching of evolution in the public schools. During the twenties, conservative Christians succeeded in introducing no less than thirty-seven anti-evolution bills into twenty state legislatures. The Scopes trial was the result of the law adopted in Tennessee.

The legal question, however, quickly became secondary to the media hoopla surrounding the trial. Clarence Darrow, the brilliant Chicago lawyer hired by the American Civil Liberties Union, defended Scopes; and William Jennings Bryan, three-time Democratic candidate for president of the United States, served as one of the prosecuting attorneys.

Both men saw the wider dimensions of the trial. Darrow stood for the values of an enlightened, scientific, liberal-minded America. Bryan defended the evangelical Protestant values of traditional, God-fearing America. The trial moved to its climax when Darrow, in the interests of intellectual freedom, succeeded in getting Bryan himself on the stand and using his own testimony to demonstrate fundamentalist stupidity. Bryan won the trial. Scopes was fined one hundred dollars. But Darrow and enlightened liberalism won in the public mind.

The trial was a dramatic symbol of the shift in American culture from small-town America, under the rule of traditional Protestant morality, to urban America, under the faith in human progress and the love of individual rights.

As we have seen, many American evangelicals, steeped in the biblical strand of culture, discovered ways to cooperate with the republican strand, and thus helped to create traditional, morally sensitive, small-town America. The economic and the therapeutic strands, however, have shaped the culture of urban America, and pose formidable resistance to the spread of the gospel in contemporary America. The twentieth-century shift in cultural ideals has left many Christians feeling like aliens in their own land. White evangelicals have joined other minorities stigmatized by faith, race, or ethnicity in wondering whether they have a share in the American Dream.

The Economic Tradition

The economic strand of American culture, rooted in the commonwealth of Puritan New England, was personified in Benjamin Franklin, an intensely practical man who dreamed of getting ahead primarily by frugality, industry, and innate shrewdness. The key word in Franklin's vocabulary was "useful." He wrote his only book, his *Autobiography*, in the expectation that it might prove useful to his son. He invented the stove, founded a hospital, paved the streets, established a city police force, all because they were useful projects. In the same way, he believed it was useful to believe in God, since God rewards virtue and punishes vice.[1]

This American faith in practicality and expediency, illustrated by Franklin, enabled Americans to stretch two threads of steel across the continent, and use the railroads to plant cities, mine the mountainsides, and turn America into an industrial giant. This pragmatic culture, with its eye on a world of possibility and gain, came to cultural dominance toward the close of the nineteenth century in the "age of big business."

At the dawn of the twentieth century it was obvious that the prevailing cultural influence in American life had shifted from the small towns, dotting the rural countryside, to the burgeoning cities, the new centers of commercial and industrial power. After 1920, when most Americans spoke of the American Dream, they meant personal, material success.

The new enthusiasm for material progress was almost omnipresent, and the common laborer and his housewife entered into the spirit of the age by securing and enjoying the products of the American industrial revolution. Mass production made possible mass consumption. After the 1920s consumer items that were once considered luxuries to the middle and lower classes were widely diffused throughout American society. Past luxuries were constantly redefined as necessities. This ascent of expectations reached the point where it seemed incredible that an ordinary product, such as a refrigerator, could ever have been considered out of the reach of an ordinary citizen.

Among these products of technological progress none were more culturally significant than the automobile and the cinema. The automobile destroyed the isolation of the small towns, which for so long had helped to guarantee a strict moral code, and the cinema, followed by television in the 1950s, brought to Americans a picture of a world far different from the one most middle-class families experienced.

Unlike the original industrial revolution in England a century earlier, the American revolution merged the nation's technical expertise with big business. The drive for maximum profits through the adoption of efficient organization moved social change into high gear. Mass marketing, for example, identified different kinds of buying groups and whetted consumer appetites; and installment buying broke down the traditional Protestant fear of debt. Thus was born America's corporate and consumer economy, the environment and expression of America's economic culture, where citizens project their rags-to-riches fantasies.[2]

By 1920 half of America's population lived in cities, the centers of production and consumption, and for many Americans the city was a different world. American industry and commerce had attracted millions of immigrants to Ellis Island in New York's harbor. Jews, Poles, Germans, Irish, Italians, and others rushed to the burgeoning cities of the nation: New York, Chicago, Boston, Philadelphia, and St. Louis. In these urban centers the traditional consensus of life in white, Protestant, moral-minded America was a thing of the past. New political power, ethnic pluralism, industrial strength, media coverage, and liberal lifestyles challenged evangelical mores. The face of American public life was changing rapidly.

Among those immigrant groups wondering about their share in the nation's glory, none was more significant than the millions of Roman Catholics. The Catholic assessment of the American Dream was complicated by the apparent conflict of the spirit of Catholicism with American values. Besieged by the forces of nationalism and liberalism in Europe after the French Revolution, the Church of Rome issued a string of pronouncements condemning democracy, the separation of church and state, and religious toleration. These left the Catholic immigrant torn between the promises of the American Dream and the Church's warnings of the nation's perils. No integrating theological case for American Catholicism came until 1965 when the Second Vatican Council issued its Declaration on Religious Freedom.

Many evangelical Protestants soon shared the Catholic's feeling of estrangement. The American Dream itself was changing. The Scopes trial was a dramatic illustration of this shift. The new gospel for America stressed happiness through change, progress, and growth. And the "bible" of the new message was Charles Darwin's *The Origin of Species*. The book's theory of evolution did not directly challenge the Scriptures' doctrines of God and creation, but popular speculation about its meaning tended to discount the traditional explanation of the origin of life and the personal God behind the universe.

Everywhere, it seemed overnight, men and women thought and spoke of evolution, process, and progress; no longer of creation, miracles, and the new birth. Evolution became the ultimate scientific justification of the innate American faith in the future.

The creed of American economic culture held not only that progress was inevitable but that the key to it was the disciplined, autonomous self, "a Promethean figure, conquering fate through sheer force of will."

This faith emerged most clearly in late nineteenth-century success ideology, which elevated the image of the self-made man. What he had in abundance were "industrious work habits, extraordinary moral discipline, and above all an indomitable will. . . . Like the heroes of Horatio Alger's novels, the self-made man would forever *Strive and Succeed*; he would always be *Struggling Upward*."[3]

The new faith in America's future found expression in a movement within Protestantism called theological liberalism, which held that Christians should adopt a sympathetic attitude toward secular culture and strive to come to terms with it. While not oblivious to the faults of modern times, liberals were confident that its basic currents were sweeping the world toward the Kingdom of God. Walter Rauschenbusch, primary spokesman for the social gospel, asserted in his *Christianity and the Social Crisis* that the kingdom "is not a matter of saving human atoms, but of saving the social organism. It is not a matter of getting individuals to heaven, but of transforming the life on earth into the harmony of heaven."

In practical terms, "transforming" America called for rebuking the laissez-faire economics of the day and replacing competitive capitalism with a more equitable social order. Most liberals expected the establishment, by evolutionary (rather than revolutionary) means, of some sort of non-Marxist democratic socialism, or at least regulated capitalism. Many of their ideals, stated in their "social creed," were later adopted as part of Franklin Roosevelt's New Deal politics.

The impact of progressivism upon the American Dream was also evident in the theological schools and Christian liberal arts colleges where professors in increasing numbers accepted a new approach to the Bible called "higher criticism." This was an attempt to employ the so-called scientific methods of literary investigation in the study of the Bible. The basic presupposition of this approach was that the Bible was a piece of literature like any other book of ancient literature, nothing more. The religious value of the Bible lay in the story of how an ancient people moved progressively from myths and folklore to new levels of religious insight and moral behavior.

Conservative Protestants saw clearly the damaging consequence of this progressive view of the gospel. It undercut the special revelation in the Bible, it left the Christian minister without a supernatural gospel to preach, and it provided no basis for the evangelical experience of the new birth. This conflict over the old-time religion of miracle and grace and the modern ideas of progress and human potential came to be called the fundamentalist-modernist controversy. On the one hand, liberals had the advantage of interpreting the rapid changes in American life in a positive light and thus gained an approving glance from American culture. On the other hand, the fundamentalists' religious convictions threw them into conflict with changing American society and made them appear outdated and irrelevant. The Scopes trial demonstrated the differences.[4]

The Therapeutic Tradition

After World War II, American society brought to prominence the fourth strand of American culture, the therapeutic.[5]

The Founding Fathers dedicated this republic to the agreeable proposition that all men, and therefore Americans especially, were endowed by their Creator with the unalienable rights of life, liberty, and the pursuit of happiness. For two hundred years Americans had tried to claim these rights, and by World War II they had generally caught up with life and liberty. But what about happiness?

In the 1840s Tocqueville concluded that the American people were "the happiest in the world." But who would dare to make such a claim today? Our pursuit of happiness carries us everywhere—to the travel agent for exotic excursions, to the drug dealer for mind-altering chemicals, to the therapist for affirmation and healing. As at no other time in our nation's history,

Americans today are in pursuit of personal happiness.

The use of "therapeutic" to identify this strand of American culture not only underscores the reverence for professional therapists in today's society but more importantly the widespread use of therapeutic ideas and language to describe or justify behavior of ordinary people. *Dysfunctional. Open up. Stressed out. Up tight.* This is the language of the age of therapy. It is thinking and speaking that reflects a view of reality stripped of the older moral categories of sin, guilt, forgiveness, and righteousness. The human need is no longer salvation; it is healing.

"For the culturally conservative image of the ascetic, enemy of his own needs," says Philip Rieff, "there has been substituted the image of the needy person, permanently engaged in the task of achieving a gorgeous variety of satisfactions."[6]

This portrait of the American Dream has many painters, but few have sold as many prints as Carl Rogers, perhaps America's most influential professional therapist. In a description of his personal development, Rogers recounts a revealing incident during his student days at New York's Union Theological Seminary. A group of students, including Rogers, wanted to pursue their own questions rather than the faculty's, so they petitioned the administration to allow them to set up their own seminar for credit. Class sessions of the seminar would address only student questions.

After the administration granted permission, the students launched the course and learned something significant about themselves. Rogers later explained:

> The majority of the members of that group, in thinking their way through the questions they had raised, thought themselves right out of religious work. I was one. I felt that questions as to the meaning of life, and the possibility of the constructive improvement of life for individuals would probably always interest me, but I could not

work in a field where I would be required to believe in some specified religious doctrine. . . . I wanted to find a field in which I could be sure my freedom of thought would not be limited.[7]

This stress on the liberation and fulfillment of the self has one striking advantage. It allows the "expressive" American to treat commitments—from marriage and work to politics and religion—not as moral obligations but as mere instruments of personal happiness.[8]

"For selfists," writes psychologist Paul Vitz, "there seem to be no acceptable duties, denials, inhibitions, or restraints. Instead, there are only rights and opportunities for change. An overwhelming number of the selfists assume there are no unvarying moral or interpersonal relationships, no permanent aspects to individuals. All is written in sand by a self in flux."[9]

The most blatant expression of this cult of self-worship lies in what is sometimes called the Sexual Revolution. Since the 1960s the highly publicized playboy philosophy has spread to the general public. Hugh Hefner, founder of *Playboy* magazine, preached for almost three decades his version of liberated sex. He argued that Americans are unhappy because they are repressed sexually. If they would simply pursue the playboy philosophy, Hefner insisted, they would find personal liberation and true happiness.

Support for the revolution came from every direction. Rock groups, movie stars, and novelists became zealous evangelists for the gospel of personal freedom. They sang and confessed the creed of the Sexual Freedom League: "We believe that sexual expression, in whatever form agreed upon between consenting persons of either sex, should be considered as an inalienable human right."

By 1980 the gospel of personal freedom for sexual expression had apparently reached the nation's general population. Pollster Daniel Yankelovich, in his book *New Rules*, revealed that Americans were becoming more tolerant of those who sought fulfillment of their sexual drives outside of marriage, including homosexuality. In 1967, 85 percent of parents of college-age youth condemned premarital sex as morally wrong. By 1979, only 37 percent did.[10]

The most important instrument in the social explosions of the last three decades was television. The changing patterns of access to information through television nurtured a host of liberation movements: blacks, women, elderly, children, disabled, animals, prisoners, renters, and others. Everyone, it seems, had discovered some "right." Television helped to change the deferential Negro into the proud Black; television merged the Miss and Mrs. into a Ms.; television transformed the child into a "human being" with natural rights. Television fostered the rise of hundreds of "minorities"—people who perceived a wider world and saw themselves as unfairly isolated in some pocket of it.[11]

As the 1960s and 1970s revealed, even federal institutions fell under the spell of the therapeutic culture. As late as 1931 in the *U.S. v. Macintosh* case the United States Supreme Court declared: "We are a Christian people according to one another the equal right of religious freedom, and acknowledging with reverence the duty of obedience to the will of God."

In the 1960s, however, the Supreme Court demonstrated a significant change in its attitude toward Christianity and traditional morality. Any lingering sense of Protestant hegemony gave way to the recognition of pluralism as the American way of life. The court permitted young men to claim exemption from military service even when their religious beliefs did not include the traditional definitions of a Supreme Being. It struck down compulsory prayers in the public schools. And it disallowed public reading of the Bible and reciting the Lord's Prayer in public schools. The climactic blow came in 1973 with the highly unpopular decision (*Roe v. Wade*) granting a woman the legal right to have an abortion.[12]

Why did the court see fit to issue these rulings? Apparently, in its eagerness to guarantee individual Americans greater and greater personal freedoms, it extended the ideal of religious pluralism, linked with the constitutional separation of church and state, to include a pluralism of *morality*. The traditional ideal of denominational pluralism was enlarged to mean *moral* pluralism. If such a shift in fact occurred, if separation of church and state has been enlarged to mean separation of morality and public life, then what universally accepted public morality remains?

As early as the 1830s Tocqueville forecast a gloomy future for this young democracy. He predicted that American individualism would one day alienate American citizens from each other to such a degree that the society would no longer be able to function. Equality, he said, tends to isolate Americans from each other, and "it lays open the soul to an inordinate love of material gratification." Many today wonder whether we have reached that point.

Can the gospel make a difference in today's America? Robert Bellah and his team believe that we still have the capacity to reconsider the course we have chosen:

> The morally concerned social movement, informed by republican and biblical sentiments, has stood us in good stead in the past and may still do so again. But we have never before faced a situation that called our deepest assumptions so radically into question. Our problems today are not just political. They are moral and have to do with the meaning of life. We have assumed that as long as economic growth continued, we could leave all else to the private sphere. Now that economic growth is faltering and the moral ecology on which we have tacitly depended is in disarray, we are beginning to understand that our common life requires

more than an exclusive concern for material accumulation.[13]

If this widely read assessment of American culture is true, then perhaps some significant role in American life remains for the Christian gospel and its moral implications for the American Dream.

FURTHER READING

Daniel Bell, *The Cultural Contradictions of Capitalism* (1976)
Robert N. Bellah and others, *Habits of the Heart* (1985)
T. J. Jackson Lears, *No Place of Grace: Antimodernism and the Transformation of American Culture 1880-1920* (1981)
Paul C. Vitz, *Psychology as Religion: The Cult of Self-Worship* (1977)

Chapter 4, Notes

1. See Daniel Bell, *The Cultural Contradictions of Capitalism* (New York: Basic Books, 1976), 57-58.
2. Ibid., 66-70.
3. T. J. Jackson Lears, *No Place of Grace: Antimodernism and the Transformation of American Culture 1880-1920* (New York: Pantheon Books, 1981), 18.
4. "A society in rapid change inevitably produces confusions about appropriate modes of behavior, taste, and dress. A socially mobile person has no ready guide for acquiring new knowledge on how to live 'better' than before, and his guides become the movies, television, and advertising. In this respect, advertising begins to play a more subtle role in changing habits than merely stimulating wants. The advertising . . . was to teach people how to dress, furnish a home, buy the right wines—in short, the styles of life appropriate to the new statuses. Though at first the changes were primarily in manners, dress, taste, and food habits, sooner or later they began to affect more basic patterns: the structure of authority in the family, the role of children and young adults as independent consumers in the society, the pattern of morals, and the different meanings of achievement in the society." Edward C. Stewart, *American Cultural Patterns: A Cross-Cultural Perspective* (LaGrange Park, Ill.: Intercultural, 1972), 69.

5. Lears, in his *No Place of Grace*, argues that therapeutic thinking arose much earlier within a movement in the 1880s called antimodernism. These were journalists, academics, ministers, and literary figures within American WASP bourgeoisie who protested the complacent progressive faith of their day. I have no reason to contest Lears's argument. I am merely stressing here the prominence of therapeutic thinking in American culture.

6. Philip Rieff, *The Triumph of the Therapeutic* (New York: Harper & Row, 1966), 241.

7. See Robert N. Sollod, "Carl Rogers and the Origins of Client-Centered Therapy" in *Professional Psychology*, February 1978, 93-104, and Paul C. Vitz, *Psychology as Religion: The Cult of Self-Worship* (Grand Rapids: Wm. B. Eerdmans Publishing Co., 1977), 76.

8. The denial of personal responsibility in the 1960s was institutionalized into various social reforms. Charles Murray of the Manhattan Institute for Policy Research has noted: "What many of these reforms shared (in varying ways and degrees) was an assumption that people are not in control of their own behavior and should not properly be held responsible for the consequences of their actions. The economic system is to blame; the social environment is to blame; perhaps accidents and conceivably genetics are to blame." His quotation is found in Charles Colson, *Kingdoms in Conflict* (Grand Rapids: Zondervan Publishing House, 1987), 77.

9. Vitz, *Psychology as Religion*, 38.

10. Daniel Yankelovich, *New Rules: Searching for Self-Fulfillment in a World Turned Upside Down* (New York: Random House, 1981), 99.

11. See Joshua Meyrowitz, *No Sense of Place: The Impact of Electronic Media on Social Behavior* (New York: Oxford University Press, 1985), 9, 309.

12. A helpful summary of court decisions since 1960 is available in *Church and State in American History*, ed. John F. Wilson and Donald L. Drakeman (Boston: Beacon Press, 1987), 223-303. The significant shift in legal thinking during the last two generations, separating legal values from religious ones, and its damaging consequences are discussed in Christopher F. Mooney, *Public Virtue* (Notre Dame, Ind.: University of Notre Dame Press, 1986), 76-80.

13. Robert N. Bellah and others, *Habits of the Heart* (New York: Harper & Row, 1985), 295.

PART 2

PUBLIC DREAMS

Since Christians experience their conflicts with contemporary American culture in both their public and their private lives, we turn in this section to three representative areas of public life where Christians are most often troubled: religious expression, political freedom, and public education. In these public areas Christians must now face the fact that they have been added to the ranks of minorities.

Chapter Five

The Public Policy of Private Faith

"There is no country in the world where the Christian religion retains a greater influence over the souls of men than in America."

—Alexis de Tocqueville in 1831

O ne of the most dramatic and often quoted descriptions of the American Dream came from a Baptist minister. In 1963 forty thousand people assembled around the pool reflecting the Lincoln Memorial in Washington to hear Dr. Martin Luther King, Jr. weave together biblical language and patriotic ideals in the highest tradition of American oratory.

Sweeping through one southern state after another—Georgia . . . Mississippi . . . Alabama—King traced his vision of a racially harmonious nation. "I have a dream," he cried, "that my little children will one day live in a nation where they will not be judged by the color of their skin but by the content of their character."

He moved on to give the dream divine sanction by quoting the messianic words of the prophet Isaiah:

"I have a dream that one day every valley shall be exalted, every hill and mountain made low . . . and the glory of the Lord will be revealed and all flesh shall see it together."

Then, after recalling the first stanza of the patriotic hymn "America," he appealed for freedom to ring across the land so that "all of God's children—black men and white men, Jews and Gentiles, Catholics and Protestants" would be able to sing, in the words of the old Negro spiritual, "Free at last, free at last; thank God Almighty, we are free at last."

Martin Luther King, Jr. saw his civil rights movement as an expression of the very best in the American Dream and "the sacred values in the Judeo-Christian heritage." In his widely circulated "Letter from Birmingham Jail," he wrote, "If today's church does not recapture the sacrificial spirit of the early church, it will lose its authenticity, forfeit the loyalty of millions, and be dismissed as an irrelevant social club with no meaning for the twentieth century." Yet even if the church should fail, the civil rights struggle will triumph, he said, because "the sacred heritage of our nation and the eternal will of God are embodied in our echoing demands."

Today's secular libertarians, who want to remove biblical religion from public life, have trouble making sense of the civil rights movement because it was so clearly a religiously inspired movement that entered the public arena and made a major difference in American life. If we deny that a biblical strand of culture even exists in American life, how can we expect to make sense of this country? Martin Luther King, Jr. demonstrated that biblical religion, even as a minority voice, has a role to play in the American Dream.[1]

Sixty years ago, in the wake of the Scopes trial, hosts of scholars, editors, entertainers, and other cultural critics thought that science and reason had completely discredited biblical religion in America. Secularity was so massive, they thought, that Christianity simply could not survive its lack of intellectual credibility and public approval. They were wrong.[2]

The American experience since World War II makes clear that all announcements of the death of biblical religion in America are gravely exaggerated. Today the "religious problem" in America is no longer concerned with whether religion will survive. It will. The question is, How will biblical faith respond to the moral and spiritual needs of the American people?

Mark Silk of the *Atlanta Constitution* recently described religion in America as a tension between the "exclusivist creeds" of Judaism and Christianity and "a spiritually inclusive national faith" that constantly appeals to our loyalty. Recalling the place of religions in the ancient Roman Empire, Silk said that Christianity and Judaism are religious faiths that "demand exclusive commitment from their devotees." In their early days any outsider who wanted to join them had to convert. He or she had to turn deliberately from indifference or another form of piety to the true faith, a turn that indicated the old way was wrong and the new way was right.

In democratic America, however, there are social pressures for a common religious faith that implies a "quasi-spiritual allegiance to the religiously impartial state." This pressure to adhere to the beliefs that are good for America—call it "civil religion" or whatever—creates the condition in which Christians and Jews live. They worship, witness, and serve in the tension between conversion and adhesion. It is a helpful way of viewing the gospel in America.[3]

Today's Private Religion

The most recent, widely accepted way to relieve this tension is to argue that religion in the United States is strictly a private matter. Any conversion, therefore, is a matter of personal choice and must be kept out of the public arena where national faith must be free to reign. This is the prevailing view in the American courts and other institutions. It is a view that interprets the constitutional "separation" of church and state to mean the separation of religion from public life, which, of course, is not the same thing.

The political use of this view—that faith is something private with no effect on public responsibilities—can be traced in recent years to the dramatic speech John F. Kennedy gave before the Houston Ministerial Association in the 1960 presidential campaign.

Many Protestants at that time feared that Kennedy, a Catholic, would be bound by the dictates of the Church of Rome. The senator from Massachusetts, however, pulled off a major political move when he told the Texas ministers, mostly Baptists, that "whatever issue may come before me as president, if I'm elected . . . I will make my decision in accordance . . . with what my conscience tells me to be in the national interest, and without regard to outside religious pressure or dictate. And no power or threat of punishment could cause me to decide otherwise."[4]

Kennedy's statement proved to be extremely popular with the Protestants in Houston, but it also set a precedent that has become a part of established American political wisdom: One's religious convictions can have no effect on one's public decisions.

The position is eminently practical, and therefore typically American. It removes the religious voice from all positions of power. But to hosts of Americans in the biblical tradition, such political schizophrenia is sheer foolishness.

When Kennedy's view first appeared in print, members of his own church called it nonsense. In a *Look* magazine article the senator had asserted that "whatever one's religion in his private life may be, for the office-holder nothing takes precedence over his oath to uphold the Constitution and all its parts." The adhesional faith of the nation apparently required no less. Upon reading Kennedy's words, however, the

Catholic magazine *America* snapped: "Mr. Kennedy doesn't really believe that. No religious man, be he Catholic, Protestant, or Jew, holds such an opinion. A man's conscience has a bearing on his public as well as his private life." The conversionist creed of Catholicism was alive, even if not completely well.[5]

The Case for Private Religion

The most widely used justification for removing traditional Christian views from public debate is what we have come to call "pluralism." The term comes from the obvious fact that religious life in America is marked by a striking diversity. It is the scholar's way of referring to the more than 250 denominations listed in the yearbooks and the 1200 religious groups alphabetized in a standard encyclopedia of American religion. Any metropolitan area's Yellow Pages will reveal the same characteristic of American life.

With so many religious bodies in the United States, how can anyone say that American culture is secular? It is secular, we discover, in the sense that America was founded on the provision of the separation of religion from public life. That, at least, is the argument. So the number of Christians in America is irrelevant to public life, because religion is a matter of personal choice; nothing more. It has been, as we say, "privatized."

This relegation of religion to the private sphere was supposedly necessary because of the intolerance of religious people. History itself was the reason that Blaise Pascal observed: "Men never do evil so completely and cheerfully as when they do it from religious conviction." Defenders of the "keep-religion-out-of-public-life" view believe that devoutly. They may not know who said it, but they know that Christians in public life were responsible for the bloody Crusades and the Inquisition. And this very intolerance, they argue, is the primary reason for the provision of separation of church and state in the Bill of Rights. In an

American society that reflects the intent of its original designers, the various churches should be on a par with each other. Each member should be free to claim his own tradition or denomination as the final embodiment of truth, but nonmembers should be under no compulsion to agree with any such claim.

Religious pluralism, then, according to this secular view of American public life, rests upon the view of the individual as an autonomous self entirely independent of any tradition or community. The American way, in this line of thinking, insists that this isolated soul has been granted the freedom of choosing any religious faith or none at all, almost as one would choose a hairstyle or a model of a car.

As a consequence, public life operates largely without moral values. "The prevailing notion," writes columnist Joseph Sobran, "is that the state should be neutral as to religion, and furthermore, that the best way to be neutral about it is to avoid all mention of it. By this sort of logic, nudism is the best compromise among different styles of dress. The secularist version of 'pluralism' amounts to theological nudism."[6]

The Traditional Place of Religion

Did the Founding Fathers intend a nation with religion and morality safely confined to the private life? Did the separation of church and state mean to them and their contemporaries the separation of religion from public life?

Certainly not! As we have seen, the enlightened Sons of Liberty and many of the Puritan-minded revivalists found common ground in the agreement that the new American government should neither establish nor interfere with the churches. The view expressed by James Madison came to prevail: "The Religion . . . of every man must be left to the conviction and conscience of every man; and it is the right of every man to exercise it as these may dictate."[7]

Does this mean, however, that biblical religion

had no role to play in American public life? The supposed constitutional separation of church and state prevented the establishment of any religion as America's state church, but it also guaranteed the free expression of religious practice. The Founding Fathers did not suggest that the republic could function without conviction, morality, or faith in the public arena.[8]

As a young man John Adams, for example, was impressed by the rationalist message of his friend Jonathan Mayhew, but he never strayed far from the Puritan belief that social law depends upon religious sanctions. During his first year as vice-president under the new Constitution (1789), Adams wrote, "We have no government armed with power capable of contending with human passions unbridled by morality and religion. Our constitution was made only for a moral and religious people. It is wholly inadequate for the government of any other."

Seven years later, when George Washington retired from public life at the end of his second term, he advised his countrymen in his farewell address to regard "religion and morality" as "indispensable supports" to "political prosperity." "Where is the security for property, for reputation, for life," he asked, "if the sense of religious obligation desert the oaths, which are the instruments of investigation in courts of justice?" Reason and experience both "forbid us to expect that national morality can prevail in exclusion of religious principle."[9]

Surely Charles Colson is right when he says, "Today's widespread relegation of religion to merely something people do only in the privacy of their homes or churches would have been unimaginable to the founders of the republic—even those who personally repudiated orthodox faith."[10]

Only a generation after the nation's founding, Tocqueville noted that religion in America "takes no direct part in the government of society, but it must be regarded as the first of their political institutions. . . . How is it possible that society should escape destruction if the moral tie is not strengthened in proportion as the political tie is relaxed? And what can be done with a people who are their own masters if they are not submissive to the Deity?"[11]

It may be possible to confine the religious faith of today's therapeutic culture to the private life, but faith as the Bible describes it reaches out to embrace all of life. The therapeutic culture offers a faith that is a psychological key to open doors into an inner world of comfort and confidence. Religion for the selfist is a matter of personal peace and freedom from stress. And that inner attitude of the soul is often called "faith."

Faith in the Bible, however, is something else. The men and women of faith we meet in the Bible are never introspective mystics, trying to work themselves into a mood of faith. On the contrary, they look away from themselves to the works of God in creation and history.

The writer of Hebrews puts it best when he declares: "Without faith it is impossible to please God, because anyone who comes to him must believe that he exists and that he rewards those who earnestly seek him."[12]

In Scripture, faith always rests on the good news of God's works in our space-time world. When Jesus urged men and women to "have faith in God," he never spoke of it as some mysterious experience that normal people find incredible. Faith, in biblical terms, is an attitude toward life open to all people. It is not something that strangely religious people pump up out of the deep recesses of their souls. It is a decision that all people make when they are confronted with convincing evidence that God has acted and revealed himself.

The Bible describes faith something like the recent television commercial that offered to the viewer the legal services of attorneys associated with a certain lawyer. We'll call him Samuel Wiseman. The announcer told how his firm cut through the legalese of the law books and offered wills, divorces, and other services at reasonable prices. Then he concluded, "I'm

Sam Wiseman. And you've got my word on it."

It was a parable of biblical faith: living with the conviction that God is as good as his Word. And by his Word Christians mean that disclosure, given to us in a special segment of history and in Scripture, about who God is and what he has done. Scripture indicates above all else that God is a Person, Someone who is. And this Someone wants us to act moment by moment on the basis of his character revealed to us in his Word. That is faith!

The fact is, then, that two conflicting convictions about the nature of faith are at the center of today's struggle for America's future. On the one hand is a radically individualistic "religion" supported by faith in some sort of unrestricted self. On the other hand is the traditional faith in the transcendent Lord of history. These are the two poles that organize much of America's spiritual life. To the first, God is simply the self magnified; to the second, God confronts men and women from outside the universe. One seeks a self that is in basic harmony with the world; the other seeks an external God who will provide order in the world, including American public life.[13]

The Christian and Public Life

Christians resist the consignment of religious faith to the private life for several very good reasons. *First*, the assumptions of the keep-religion-out-of-public-life people have deadly consequences. If selves are defined by their preferences, but those preferences are completely arbitrary, then each self constitutes its own moral and religious universe. There is no conclusive way to reconcile conflicting claims about what is good. In the absence of any transcendent standard of right and wrong, good or evil, the self and its feelings become our only moral guide.[14]

Robert Bellah and his associates found the prize example of privatized religion in a young nurse named Sheila Larson. "I believe in God," she reported. "I'm not a religious fanatic. I can't remember the last time I went to church. My faith has carried me a long way. It is Sheilaism. Just my own little voice. . . . It's just try to love yourself and be gentle with yourself. You know, I guess, take care of each other. I think He would want us to take care of each other."[15]

Second, most Christians hold, along with Richard John Neuhaus, that the naked public square will not remain naked. If the traditional Jewish-Christian case for transcendent standards for American public life is rejected, something else will move into the sanitized space. Human beings are incurably religious, and their political life never remains neutral.

When Donald Regan, former chief of staff in the Reagan White House, revealed in his book *For the Record* that the Reagans often scheduled important presidential events according to astrological predictions, the American people gasped in shock. "I don't know about you," wrote Tom Teepen of the *Atlanta Constitution*, "but I don't find it entirely comforting that the man with one hand on The Button has the other on a crystal ball." Teepen, like most of us, had hoped for more enlightened leadership, but it is an example of what can happen when we try to keep the Almighty out of public life.

A generation ago the Roman Catholic scholar, John Courtney Murray, asked how many and what kinds of religious groups can a republic tolerate and still function? His question reflects the Christian conviction that American society needs certain sets of values like those historically associated with Jewish and Christian religion.

Third, while religion has often been linked with oppressive regimes, and our Founding Fathers had the good sense to guard against such a development in the United States, it is also true that nonreligious regimes can be oppressive. Have we forgotten the meaning of Stalinism? What about the French Revolution? These are bloody examples of thoroughly secular governments' attempts to govern without regard for the religious needs of people.

When the state attempts to confine religion to the private sphere, it soon reveals totalitarian inclinations to oppress religion. And that is what we have seen in recent years in the United States. The church's rights to express itself, and to conduct its own affairs, have been insidiously eroded.

The Collinsville, Oklahoma, case is one of the better examples. A thirty-six-year-old nurse, Marian Guinn, sued her church for invasion of privacy because it disciplined her for fornication with Pat Sharpe, the local druggist and former mayor. The court ruled in her favor and awarded her $390,000. Clearly in this case the judicial system restricted the right of the church to express itself in a matter of institutional discipline. If the United States government can penalize a church for doing what churches have always done, what does the free exercise clause of the Bill of Rights mean?[16]

What is the conclusion of the whole matter? Neuhaus has summarized it best. He has argued that the real danger to America lies not in a conspiracy led by "secular humanists"—as the Christian Right often claims—but in "the pervasive influence of ideas about a secular society and a secular state, ideas that have insinuated themselves also into our religious thinking and have been institutionalized in our politics."[17]

Today, the state poses a much greater danger than the church of upsetting the constitutional balance between republican government and religious freedom, because people have come to equate the state with society itself. The answer lies with Christians who, even as a dedicated minority, will clearly affirm our democratic governance and bear witness to "the transcendent purpose to which society is held accountable." We dare to claim this new mission for Christians, because as early as 1963, Martin Luther King, Jr. and his civil rights movement demonstrated for the whole country the power of a dedicated minority.[18]

FURTHER READING

Richard John Neuhaus, *The Naked Public Square*
(1984)
A. James Reichley, *Religion in American Public Life*
(1985)
Mark Silk, *Spiritual Politics* (1988)

Chapter 5, Notes

1. "As a legacy of our religious traditions, ground swells of religious moralism have periodically emerged in American politics. In the mid to late nineteenth century, for example, religion had injected moral issues into our political dialogue. The abolition of slavery, prohibition, blue laws, and teaching the Bible in the class-room had become the leading political issues of the day." The "possibility of moral issues finding political expression remains a recurrent theme in American politics." *Connecticut Mutual Life Report on American Values in the '80s: The Impact of Belief* (Hartford, Conn.: Connecticut Mutual Life Insurance Co., 1981), 9.

2. See Anthony T. Padovano, *American Culture and the Quest for Christ* (New York: Sheed & Ward, 1970), 115.

3. See Mark Silk, *Spiritual Politics* (New York: Simon and Schuster, 1988), 19-20.

4. Charles Colson, *Kingdoms in Conflict* (Grand Rapids: Zondervan Publishing House, 1987), 284.

5. Silk, *Spiritual Politics*, 119-20.

6. Joseph Sobran, "Pensees: Notes for the Reactionary of Tomorrow," *National Review*, 31 December 1985, 48.

7. Found in Edwin S. Gaustad, ed., *A Documentary History of Religion in America* (Grand Rapids: Wm. B. Eerdmans Publishing Co., 1982), 1:262.

8. The expression "a wall of separation" between church and state came informally from Jefferson. It is not in the Constitution itself.

9. See A. James Reichley, *Religion in American Public Life* (Washington, D.C.: The Brookings Institution, 1985), 102-5.

10. Colson, *Kingdoms in Conflict*, 121.

11. Alexis de Tocqueville, *Democracy in America*, trans. George Lawrence, ed. J. P. Mayer (New York: Doubleday, Anchor Books, 1969), 292.

12. Hebrews 11:6.

13. See Robert N. Bellah and others, *Habits of the Heart* (New York: Harper & Row, 1985), 235.

14. Ibid., 76.

15. Ibid., 221.

16. See Colson, *Kingdoms in Conflict*, 206-8.

17. Richard John Neuhaus, *The Naked Public Square* (Grand Rapids: Wm. B. Eerdmans Publishing Co., 1984), 112-13.

18. Ibid., 116.

Chapter Six

The Right to Life and Liberty

"No man is free who is a slave to the flesh."
—Seneca, the emperor Nero's first-century tutor.

*T*he ten blocks surrounding Eighth Avenue and 44th Street in New York City are the center of the city's multi-billion dollar sex industry. Signs on the storefronts advertise peep shows of sexual perversion, and on the sidewalks prostitutes, in their form-fitting skirts, lounge around open doorways.

Late in the 1960s, in this "rotten core of the Big Apple," Franciscan priest Father Bruce Ritter opened Covenant House, a crisis center for runaway children. He knew that the molesters who ran the sex industry and the junkies who dealt the drugs operated off bodies of these twelve- and thirteen-year-old chi And he knew that many of the children wante

"It was a pretty bloody mess," said Father Ritter. "We had hundreds of distraught kids coming, really wiped-out youngsters, most of them exploited, a lot of them into drugs. Many of them died, some jumped out of windows, some were killed, some went back home."

By 1980 Covenant House had spread to ten other locations around the city and had gained a reputation of care for the casualties of the urban jungle. Over fifteen thousand kids found the crisis center a way station to a better life: food, shelter, protection from their pimp, schooling, a job, and a chance to go home. Covenant House came to stand for hope on a dead-end street called "Freedom." In that sense it may be a symbol of Christian ministry in the near future.[1]

In prevailing American culture the magic term *freedom* captures our dreams of happiness in both our personal and our political lives. It is probably, as Robert Bellah and his associates claim, "the most resonant, deeply held American value."

But what do we mean by freedom and what is the basis for it in American civil life? These are the questions that reveal today's confrontation between the advocates of a morality of personal choice and defenders of a biblically based civic morality.

American Freedom

Both sides in this debate appeal to the founding documents of America and to the prestige of the Founding Fathers. Both sides know that the civil liberties expressed in the Bill of Rights have made America's republican culture a light of freedom for peoples around the world for two centuries.

rs, however, Americans in increas-
come to think of the rights of "life,
ursuit of happiness" almost exclu-
lividual rights and benefits. Secular
erapeutic Age insists that freedom
onditions in American society that
l happiness and freedom from all

religious superstition, all social tyranny, and all moral constraint.

This secularist gospel claims that every individual has the innate authority to choose what is best for herself. "So away with every restrictive law of society," say the civil libertarians. "I ought to be able to see and say and smoke and wear what I please." This is freedom in the Therapeutic Age.

Christians, however, along with their fellow citizens in the biblical tradition, know that this gospel of personal liberties—freedom without moral constraints or civil responsibilities—was not what the Founding Fathers had in mind.

For example, James Madison wrote, "I go on this great republican principle, that the people will have virtue and intelligence to select men of virtue and wisdom." He then went on to ask, "Is there no virtue among us? If there be not, no form of government can render us secure. To suppose that any form of government will secure liberty or happiness without virtue in the people is a chimerical idea."[2]

While the Constitution itself imposes no religious test for public office, there is abundant evidence that the Founding Fathers recognized that if the American experiment in democracy was to succeed, a religious and moral people was an absolute necessity.

Many informed Americans recognize that the American form of government rests upon an intelligent appraisal of human nature. When the Treaty of Paris ended the Revolution in 1783 and secured American independence, James Madison and his Federalist colleagues struggled to achieve a new equilibrium of liberty and order. Madison defended a republican form of government precisely because he recognized that "the latent causes of faction" were "sown in the nature of man." Human beings, he wrote, are "disposed to vex and oppress each other" rather than to cooperate for their common good. That is why, he felt, a republican form of government was necessary. Representatives with "enlightened views" and "virtuous sentiments" could control the effects of factious interests.[3]

The American government, then, rests upon a view of human nature rooted in the biblical tradition, which thousands of years ago underscored the dangers of the cult of personality. It recognizes that each of us is a potential tyrant. Each of us has that seed, that arrogance, that selfishness, that authoritarian instinct in us. The aim of the Founding Fathers was to create a structure that checks this factious spirit and permits each of us to pursue life, liberty, and happiness within reasonable, civil limits.

James Bryce, writing almost a century after the Constitution was drafted, concluded, "There is a hearty Puritanism in the view of human nature that pervades the instrument of 1787. It is the work of men who believed in original sin, and were resolved to leave open for transgressors no door which they could possibly shut. Compare this spirit with the enthusiastic optimism of the Frenchmen of 1789. It is not merely a difference of race temperaments: it is a difference of fundamental ideas."[4]

This view of human nature running through the Constitution throws significant light upon American liberties today. Since human beings reveal a destructive self-interest, individual anarchy is simply unacceptable in a civil society. Our "own thing" must be restrained by considerations of the public interest. As John Locke once expressed it, "Where law ends, tyranny begins." To enjoy freedom, then, we must have a system of restraints and order in society.[5]

Secular-minded libertarians in this Age of Therapy are inclined to ignore this moral context of American freedom. But given our history, how can we?

In the summer of 1986 Americans celebrated the rededication of the Statue of Liberty. The celebration, mixing civic pride, tradition, and garish Hollywood entertainment, often overshadowed the message of F. A. Bartholdi's refurbished architecture. The Lady in the harbor is a heroic image in metal and stone of true liberty: a woman, not a warrior, quietly confident. In one hand Liberty holds the torch of freedom and in the other the tablet of law. The torch challenges the forces of darkness and tyranny. The tablet of law reminds us that liberty degenerating into license is but another form of slavery. True freedom for others is only possible in a community of civic virtue.

Early visitors to American shores detected this unusual alliance of private character and public morality. In 1837, for example, the Austrian journalist Francis Grund wrote, "The religious habits of the Americans form not only the basis of their private and public morals, but have become so thoroughly interwoven with their whole course of legislation that it would be impossible to change them without affecting the very essence of their government."[6]

That is the whole point. Recent advocates of "individual rights," freedom without religious or moral constraints, have tried to introduce significant changes into the very essence of American government.

To cite just one example, in his *Kingdoms in Conflict* Charles Colson notes the widespread belief in America today that public debate should be free of any religious influence. He then recounts the experience of Congressman Henry Hyde.

In 1976 Congress passed the Hyde Amendment, which barred federal funds for abortions in the Medicaid program. Planned Parenthood, the ACLU, and other groups challenged the amendment's constitutionality, claiming it imposed "a peculiarly religious view of when a human life begins." To prove their theory, the plaintiffs' lawyers asked to review Hyde's mail for expressions of religious sentiment—such as the suspicious use of "God bless you" at the end of a letter. Their private investigator even followed Hyde to a mass for the unborn and took notes as the congressman read Scripture, took communion, and prayed.

The plaintiffs later testified that these observations evidenced a simmering religious conspiracy. Hyde, they argued, a devout Catholic, could not separate his religion from his politics, and the Hyde Amendment was thus unconstitutional.

This secularist view of American law arises from a particular and significant use of rights. These rights are not those conferred by Providence, positive law, or custom on specific classes of people. No, these rights supposedly are the exclusive property of individual human beings. They are often cited as reason for holding that society has no right to interfere with a person's pursuit of life, liberty, and happiness.

In this social relativism all values are equal. Everyone should be allowed to decide truth for himself. Religion is a private matter and ought to be expelled from any public debate. So, as is true in totalitarian regimes, both fascist and communist, the moral voice of the churches and synagogues is consigned to political and cultural silence.

The rights, however, to which the American patriots appealed did not rest on laws created by human governments. They were inherent and valid because they were based on the ancient theory of natural law. They bore divine sanction. The English legal writer Blackstone, who was widely read in early America, once said, "This law of nature . . . dictated by God himself, is of course superior in obligation to any other. . . . No human laws are of any validity if contrary to this." These were the rights "endowed by the Creator" that became the basis of the American constitutional government.[7]

That, of course, is not the view of rights commonly held in our own time. Rights today are supposed to be positive and without obligation—rights to due process, to education, to child care, to a decent wage, to choose an abortion, to adopt the homosexual lifestyle. They are most often called "human rights" and are supposed to belong to all individuals, whatever their sex, race, religion, talents, or deserts—and without any reference to God. The truth is plain, writes ethicist Alasdair MacIntyre, "there are no such rights, and belief in them is one with belief in witches and in unicorns."[8]

This then, says Richard John Neuhaus, i... tural crisis in America: the popularly accepted systems of the Judeo-Christian tradition are larg... excluded from the public arena in which the decisions are made about how the society should be ordered. If courts persist in systematically ruling out of order the moral traditions in which Western law has developed and which bear, for the overwhelming majority of the American people, a living sense of right and wrong, then we can look forward to a continuing and deepening crisis. "The result, quite literally, is the outlawing of the basis of law."[9]

The proposition that America is a secular society, in the sense that libertarians often use the term, is simply contrary to sociological fact. Hence millions of Americans, Neuhaus argues, "have for a long time felt put upon. Theirs is a powerful resentment against values that they believe have been imposed upon them, and an equally powerful sense of outrage at the suggestion that they are the ones who pose the threat of undemocratically imposing values upon others."[10]

In 1987, Denver Catholic Archbishop J. Francis Stafford published a thirty-six-page pastoral letter called "This Home of Freedom." In it he offered praise for the nation's past but sharp criticism of what we have called our therapeutic culture:

> How does one evaluate a society in which 40% of marriages end in divorce, in which millions of innocents die in abortions, in which hundreds of thousands are born out of wedlock, and in which virtually every imaginable "lifestyle" is culturally affirmed . . . no matter what its moral, psychological, or social consequences? How shall we read the moral temperature of a society and culture in which the abuse of drugs and alcohol testifies to a pervasive loneliness amidst mobility and informality, and in which permanence of commitment often takes a back seat to the next available thrill?[11]

...e millions of other Christians, detect-
...n the moral sickness in American soci-
...vasive insistence upon personal rights.
...al conduct in government, on Wall
...n the media recalls the lines from
...e:

Vice is a monster of so frightful mien,
As to be hated needs but to be seen;
Yet seen too oft, familiar with her face,
We first endure, then pity, then embrace.

Christians resist the removal of religious and
moral standards from public life in favor of a morality
of personal choice for two basic reasons: they hold to
the biblical meaning of freedom and to an objective
basis of freedom.

The Meaning of Freedom

Christians know that when the Bible speaks of
freedom it has something other than individual rights
in mind. Instead of a philosophy of individual liberties
based on some wonderful me, just below the surface
of public impressions, the Bible insists that we will
never know true freedom until we acknowledge God's
authority and purpose in our lives.

If we go through life looking for the experience or
the person or the trip that will open us up and set us
free—the condition that will make us unbelievably
happy—then we are headed for heartache, not happiness. Personal freedom is not in some outward cir-
cumstance so much as it is in the condition of the
soul.

That idea comes from no less an authority than
Jesus Christ. During one of his dialogues with certain
Jewish leaders, Jesus promised, "If you hold to my
teaching, you are really my disciples. Then you will
know the truth, and the truth will set you free."

The Jewish leaders responded, "We are Abraham's descendants and have never been slaves of any-

one. How can you say that we shall be set free?"

"I tell you the truth," said Jesus, "everyone who sins is a slave to sin. Now a slave has no permanent place in the family, but a son belongs to it forever. So if the Son sets you free, you will be free indeed."[12]

The significant mark of Jesus' invitation to freedom, then, was a call to acknowledge the authority of Almighty God. The truth that sets people free is the truth that comes from discovering God's purpose in life.

As long as we think of freedom as freedom from restraints, we are in danger of a self-destructive pride. Human beings find fulfillment not in their vain attempts to find happiness by experiencing every exotic drink or place or pleasure, but in the communion and burden of a shared goal. Jesus indicated that genuine freedom is found in the discovery of life with a purpose.

In his *Foolishness to the Greeks*, Lesslie Newbigin indicates that long after World War II vast numbers of Britons considered the best years of their lives to be those years during the war when they shared the bombing of cities, the destruction of homes, the shortages of food, and the constant threat of death. The memory that colored the whole dark picture was the shared commitment to a common cause.

The opposite is also tragically true. When the public life of a people lacks any accepted vision of a shared goal, and every individual is free to pursue his self-chosen pleasures, the nation is in danger—not from external destruction but from death within.

The importance of purpose is all around us. Birds are made to swoop and soar; we don't expect to see them diving under water to feed on algae. Confined under water, they die. Freedom for birds is found in accepting the limits of the open skies, the purpose for which they were designed.

The Christian gospel makes the same point. Men and women in search of freedom will find only slavery to others' opinions or to the symbols of success until they find life's purpose in the True One who has come from God.

The Basis of Freedom

The gospel story of Jesus' spirited conversation with the Jewish leaders makes clear that Jesus recognized, just as American culture does, the centrality of personal choice in our freedom. Jesus, however, in a way that American culture often ignores, pressed the question of the basis of our choices. If we define the self by its ability to choose its own values, on what grounds do we make those choices?

In recent American culture, "the right act" is often simply the one that provides the most exciting challenge or the most positive feeling. But that is life without moral guidelines. If selves are defined by their preferences but those preferences are arbitrary, then each self constitutes its own moral universe. How do responsible authorities in society ever determine what is good in itself? Without objective standards of right and wrong, good or evil, the self and its feelings become our only moral guide.[13]

Most Americans in an earlier day saw that you cannot build a republic on such shifting sands. Leader after leader in America—from John Winthrop to Benjamin Franklin to Abraham Lincoln to Martin Luther King, Jr.—has taught the importance of moral character in the pursuit of the American experiment. They understood that a republic, and especially a democratic republic, must be a community of virtue. "A kingdom has subjects, not citizens; in a kingdom, it can be sufficient for the conduct of public life that the king be virtuous. In a republic, on the other hand, virtuous citizens are essential."[14]

Today's popular law-unto-itself life-style is simply not a form of freedom the American founders would recognize. It is a form of slavery to the approval of peers. Alexis de Tocqueville saw this. He once remarked that when a person no longer relies upon tradition or authority, he inevitably looks to others for confirmation of his judgments: "Refusal to accept established opinion and anxious conformity to the opinions of one's peers turns out to be two sides of the same coin."[15]

Jesus suggested the same need for moral standards when he said, "Everyone who sins is a slave to sin." He was not suggesting that a single act of sin is enslaving, but a choice of direction in life, a determination to do my own thing at all costs, is. That, says Jesus, leads to slavery.

The path to freedom, then, is in our commitments. The famous nineteenth-century historian Lord Acton once wrote that freedom is "not the power of doing what we like, but the right of being able to do what we ought." He was right. In America this means the freedom to worship, to serve others, to develop the human spirit. In a word, true freedom begins with God.

That brings us back to Father Ritter's Covenant House, a center of hope on a dead end street. It may be a model for Christian ministry in the near future. While we would like to think that Christians could bring America back to the biblical values of an earlier day, this may not prove possible. The Bible makes no promise that the United States will always be shaped by Christian values. The day of Christian ministry as a minority is upon us. That means that Christians must face their share of unpopularity and sacrifice. But it also means that we have unlimited opportunities, like Covenant House, to bring true freedom and hope to the countless casualties of today's "freedom without limits."

FURTHER READING

Christopher F. Mooney, *Public Virtue* (1986)
Mark A. Noll, *One Nation Under God? Christian Faith and Political Action in America* (1988)
Kenneth D. Wald, *Religion and Politics in the United States* (1987)

Chapter 6, Notes

1. Kenneth L. Wilson, "At the Rotten Core of the Big Apple," *World Vision*, September 1979, 6-9.
2. Theodore Draper, "Hume and Madison: The Secrets of *Federalist Paper* No. 10," *Encounter* 58 (1982):47, cited in Robert N. Bellah and others, *Habits of the Heart* (New York: Harper & Row, 1985).
3. See Madison's *Federalist Paper 10*.
4. Quoted in A. James Reichley, *Religion in American Public Life* (Washington, D.C.: The Brookings Institution, 1985), 105-6.
5. See ibid., 93.
6. Quoted in Richard John Neuhaus, *The Naked Public Square* (Grand Rapids: Wm. B. Eerdmans Publishing Co., 1984), 202-3.
7. See Samuel Eliot Morison, *The Oxford History of the American People* (New York: Oxford University Press, 1965), 272.
8. Alasdair MacIntyre, *After Virtue: A Study in Moral Theory* (Notre Dame, Ind.: University of Notre Dame Press, 1981), 66-67. See also Christopher F. Mooney, *Public Virtue* (Notre Dame, Ind.: University of Notre Dame Press, 1986), 76-80.
9. Neuhaus, *Naked Public Square*, 258-59.
10. Ibid., 52.
11. J. Francis Stafford, "This Home of Freedom: A Pastoral Letter to the Church of Denver," 28 May 1987, 9.
12. John 8:31-36.
13. See Bellah, *Habits of the Heart*, 76.
14. Stafford, "Freedom," 10-11.
15. See Bellah, *Habits of the Heart*, 148.

Chapter Seven

Opening and Closing the American Mind

"A mind, like a parachute, is only useful when it is open."
—An American bumper sticker in the 1980s

*D*uring a visit to a high school in the late seventies, sociologist Gerald Grant noticed a teacher who was visibly upset about a group of students who had verbally assaulted her and made sexually degrading comments in the hallway. When he asked why she didn't report the episode, she responded, "Well, it wouldn't have done any good."

"Why not?" he inquired.

"I didn't have any witnesses," she replied.

Adult authority, as Grant noted later, was reduced to what would stand up in court![1]

American high schools were a significant part of the social revolution that broke over the United States in the sixties and seventies, and were profoundly changed in ways that added hosts of Christian voices to the chorus of critics. In his book *The World We Created at Hamilton High 1953-1987*, Grant presents a true-to-life case study of the destruction of the peaceful world of those "happy days" on the American high school campus in the fifties as the cultural revolution of the sixties and seventies swept over the country.

Grant, professor of Cultural Foundations of Education and Sociology at Syracuse University, calls the school Hamilton High in Median, U.S.A., but it is in fact Nottingham High in Syracuse, New York. The school opened its doors in 1953 in a middle-class residential neighborhood. During its early years Hamilton reflected its setting—high achievement and social conformity.

Twenty years later pimps moved about the school grounds, the principal had a full-time bodyguard, and school closings due to violence were commonplace. Grant is persuaded that Hamilton's difficulties reflect the problems of urban public high schools across the country.

According to Grant, the dramatic changes at Hamilton can be traced directly to a string of reforms designed to guarantee high school students the legal rights of adults. During the very years that new societal goals—desegregation, mainstreaming handicapped students, and due process for students—were introduced to American high schools, the moral order within the schools themselves plummeted.

As a result, Hamilton High dumped all thoughts of itself as a traditional academic community responsible to impart moral values to the student along with information and skills. Cheating spread throughout the school. The drug counselor on campus claimed to be unqualified to tell students what is right and wrong. And teachers made no attempt to impose discipline or to tell students how to live. In short, Hamilton became a bureaucratic, utilitarian institution where people got what they wanted and moved on.

This demise of moral authority was central to the

"negative ethos" in public schools. In the fifties, Grant says, principals and teachers ran schools through the exercise of traditional authority that went with their jobs. The sixties and seventies, however, swept away the old relationships, built on years of informal consensus, and in their place stood the new legal "equality." Teachers, says Grant, "were placed in the paradoxical position of being asked to socialize their equals."[2]

By the mid-eighties teachers and students at Hamilton had reached "a negotiated reality." The harsh adversarial tone of the seventies was a thing of the past, but there was no return to the fifties. Life at Hamilton High became an academic model of education in a therapeutic culture. While students deplored Hamilton's lack of respect, absence of caring, and hostility, they celebrated their individuality and diversity and resented any attempt of a faculty member "to pry into my personal life or to interfere."

What Is Wrong with Our Schools?

Grant's criticism of American public education has become a familiar story. Schools are not lacking reformers with their special agendas for change. The American school system is, after all, an enormous enterprise. There are approximately forty-five million students attending more than ninety thousand schools, under the supervision of roughly two million teachers, at a cost, each year, in excess of eighty billion dollars. The day of private tutorials is virtually gone. Today's school systems have many constituents—parents, publishers, teachers, politicians, labor unions, state administrators—and nearly all of them have their own ideas about what ought to be done to improve the educational system.

Such criticism is understandable given education's vital role in a democracy. It is one of the primary conveyers of the ideas, culture, and fundamental beliefs of a people. It influences the intellectual and moral character of future generations. Nothing a society does requires more obvious appeal to moral values. Naturally, religious people of all shades have a profound interest in the conduct of education in America. Why shouldn't they be concerned about the recent moral crises in education, AIDS information, teen pregnancies, and control of the traffic in drugs? Do we really believe that American education can operate in a value-free secular environment?

In the last forty years hosts of Protestant Christians have joined the critics of public education. They know that schools are the center of cultural change, and much of what we become as a nation is shaped on the schoolyards of America. Their concern focuses on the breathtaking decline of traditional values. They contend that the schools no longer prepare students for responsible citizenship in a democracy or address the moral standards essential for family life and a truly civil society.

Christians know that the Bible nowhere describes the character of education in a democracy, but it does make clear that parents are responsible before God to bring up their children "in the training and instruction of the Lord." And many Christians recall that as late as the 1950s parents could count on the support and cooperation of the public school system in fulfilling that obligation. Not so today.

Today's substitutes for traditional morality can be found in two practices. The first is what Robert Bellah calls *therapeutic contractualism*—styles of interaction based on therapeutic language and the "human relations" style of management. Therapeutic contractualism encourages the view that if a student gets into trouble, he has a psychological problem that must be dealt with in a therapeutic relationship. No fault lies with the school or community for its failure to teach morality.[3]

The second is *values clarification*. This process, according to Sidney B. Simon, who popularized the method, "involves knowing what one prizes, choosing those things which one cares for most, and weaving those things into the fabric of daily living." Teachers of values clarification stress that values are different, but none is better or more adequate than another.

Critics of the process, including many Christians, charge that the method breeds absolute relativism among students. But it has also produced coercive peer pressure to adopt the most popular choice of values.[4]

How did we ever arrive at this highly questionable state of affairs? The answer, of course, lies in the story of public education in America. If we trace the major shifts in American education, we will be able to understand the recent attitude many Christians have toward public schools and the options they have for action.

Traditional Education

The treatment of religious values in American public schools has gone through three overlapping stages. First, there was an evangelical Protestant period. Second, there was a brief period of nondenominational religious emphasis. Finally, there is the current period of secular education.

The story of traditional public education could begin at many points, but none is more revealing than the year 1848 when the Reverend George H. Atkinson, a graduate of Andover Theological School and a Congregational minister, arrived in Oregon as a missionary for the American Home Missionary Society. His assignment was to create "churches, schools, whatever would benefit humanity—temperance, virtue, the industrial, mental, moral, and religious training of the young, and the establishment of society upon sound principles by means of institutions and religion and learning."

Within two years Atkinson had persuaded Oregon's Governor Joseph Lane to establish a public school system, drafted the governor's message to the legislature on that subject, written the basic legislation, seen it adopted by the state legislature and signed into law by the governor, and been appointed the first school commissioner from Clackamas County. By the time he died in 1889 Atkinson was widely credited with being the father of the public elementary school in Oregon.

No one thought it strange that Atkinson, in addition to his work in public education, also founded private "sectarian" academies in Oregon and Washington. Most Americans did not perceive any sharp distinction between public and private schools. The values of Protestant churches were also the values of public education. And not many people cared to challenge the fact.[5]

Most nineteenth-century Americans thought that moral and religious values belonged in the classroom. Thomas Jefferson's charter of government for the western states maintained that since "religion, morality and knowledge" were "necessary to good government and the happiness of mankind, schools and the means of education shall forever be encouraged." With widespread social backing, biblical morality became an integral part of early republican culture.[6]

It is easy to trace the outline of this moral order through the pages of the *McGuffey Readers*, 120 million copies of which were sold between 1839 and 1920. The moral values of nineteenth-century evangelical Protestants are found in the *Readers*: industry, obedience to parents, kindness to old folks and animals, temperance, generosity, promptness, and the inevitable triumph of the virtuous over the wicked, for, as Henry Steele Commager puts it, "Behind the great unknown, standeth God within the shadows, keeping watch above His own."[7]

Many European visitors noted this alliance between republican culture and Protestant values in traditional American education. The sympathetic Francis Grund observed this blending when he wrote, "Who upon entering an American school-room and witnessing the continual exercise in reading and speaking, or listening to the subject of their discourses, and watching the behavior of the pupils toward each other and their teachers, could, for a moment, doubt his being amongst a congregation of young republicans?"[8]

The first significant threat to this nineteenth-century educational world came with the millions of immigrants who began arriving on American shores midway through the century. The nation's compulsory education laws were in place by the time the millions of Roman Catholics arrived in New York harbor. Fears soon spread, however, that "politically backward elements" from Europe might introduce regressive old-world patterns of government into the United States. In this climate the responsibility for preparing hosts of immigrants for life in America was never far from the schoolhouse steps. Education came to stand for "Americanization."

It became increasingly evident, however, that Roman Catholics wanted no part of the Protestant values in American public schools. The Third Plenary Council of Baltimore in 1884 adopted the dictum, "Every Catholic child in a Catholic school." The mandate stood for a hundred years. From 1860 to 1960 close to 90 percent of all children in private schools in America were enrolled in Catholic parochial schools.

While proponents of equality in America resisted this alternative Catholic school system, backers of freedom of choice defended it. And the voice for freedom won. As the nation became more and more pluralistic with the landing of each immigrant ship, reformer after reformer called for a nondenominational value system in the public schools.

One of the more influential sponsors of the move was Horace Mann, the secretary of the Massachusetts Board of Education in the 1840s. Mann was himself a religious-minded person, a Unitarian, who showed a distinct preference for a Judeo-Christian approach to values. He urged the "daily use of the Bible in school" along with teaching the great principles of "natural religion."

By the end of the nineteenth century other educational reformers were pushing the nondenominational movement one step further and advocating the secularization of the public schools. In 1899 John Dewey wrote *The School and Society*, arguing for the elimination of all religious teaching in the public schools. A revolution was brewing. In 1918 the U.S. Bureau of Education published its famous *Cardinal Principles of Secondary Education*. Among its seven objectives was the development of "ethical character" but without religious training.

Little by little progressive reformers, calling for the elimination of all religion, had their way. The 1962 Supreme Court decision that declared prayer in public schools unconstitutional marked the end of the era of traditional Protestant values in American public education.[9]

We now know what filled the vacuum. As Grant's study and others show, step by step the vestiges of religion and morality were removed from campuses, and criticism of traditional values became common. Various social movements, working through "student rights," created a "new morality." In a major expansion of the traditional concept of "socialization," school officials brought the family's work to school. Life adjustment, sex education, independent living, health care, single parenting, and a host of other services were offered in a supposed morally neutral environment.

The church and the family, the other two institutions of cultural transmission that might be expected to counter this trend in America's therapeutic culture, have instead been shaped in its image. Too often they even justify their capitulation on the ground that they serve the society best when they provide a mirror reflection of it.

Where Christians Feel the Rub

Conservative Christians—often labeled "fundamentalists" in the media—are the major exception to the widespread compromise with secular culture. When public school values were Protestant, a vigorous Roman Catholic school system emerged. Now that public school values are secular, a strong Protestant private school movement has appeared. During the last thirty years the Catholic school population has declined significantly while the non-Catholic private school population may have tripled or even quadrupled.[10]

Just how do these conservative Christians resist the ideals and policies of recent public education in America? Beneath the headlines about "creation" in the science classroom and the occult in the literature assignment, what are the basic issues that trouble Christians?

First, contrary to their cultural image since the Scopes trial, Christians are not the enemies of truth, they are its defenders. One of the primary reasons for their criticisms of the public schools today is that truth is no longer valued.

In 1987 classicist Allan Bloom argued in his widely read book, *The Closing of the American Mind*, that today's university student believes one thing deeply. It has reached the status of an axiom. He is absolutely convinced that truth is relative, and he is astonished if anyone is foolish enough to challenge the point.

This relativism is not the product of theoretical reasoning. It is, so the student believes, a moral postulate of a free society. He has been taught from childhood that the danger of absolutism is not error but intolerance. Thus in our democratic society, says Bloom, openness is the highest virtue. It makes possible our American pluralism, "regardless of race, color, sex, or creed." In the past, wars, slavery, racism, persecution, and chauvinism were the products of men and women who thought they alone were right. But the past is only prelude. We have now discovered that to correct past mistakes and be right is not the supreme insight; no, the supreme insight is not to think you are right at all. We must be open to all kinds of life-styles, all ideologies. In such a society, the arch-enemy is the person who is not open to everything, the man or woman who truly believes.

Christianity, however, teaches that the historicity of a divine revelation is the cornerstone of truth. It insists upon the hard, factual quality of truth—upon a string of events, a birth in Bethlehem, a body upon a cross, an empty tomb.

Charles Colson, former White House aide turned evangelical, is only one example of the many questioning Christians. In his *Kingdoms in Conflict*, he charges that in the last generation American universities became centers of political activism and defenders of relativism, rather than centers in search of the truth. He recalls that as early as 1940 the influential theologian Reinhold Niebuhr raised the question of truth and warned that America was a victim of "an education adrift in relativity that doubted all values, and a degraded science that shirked the spiritual issues."[11] Says Colson, "Where once the object of learning had been the discovery of truth, now each student must be allowed to decide truth for himself. Dogma, not ignorance, became the enemy."[12]

Second, Christians insist that education, like public life in general, simply cannot operate in a moral vacuum. In a democracy education does not long survive without morality. While Christians admire the Enlightenment's emphasis on the use of reason and the pursuit of truth, they know that education alone is no guarantee of civility. Education cannot operate without moral standards.

Christians challenge the idea that education as it is currently pursued in America will be able to cure society's ills. In any democratic society education has a role to play. Fears feed on ignorance and an informed citizenry is basic to the ballot. But education without transcendent standards can only develop what is latent. It cannot change human nature. It can make a saint into an intelligent believer; or it can make a thief into a crafty burglar. It can teach the young to read the classics or to pour over pornography.

Christians, therefore, understand profoundly the social observer William Raspberry when he challenges the widespread belief that information alone will solve America's social problems. In April 1987, Raspberry, columnist for the *Washington Post*, asked, "What is the cure for stupidity?"

He was referring to the drug epidemic in America, and took note of the athlete-celebrities who volunteer their time on television to warn kids about the dangers of drugs. But they might as well save their million-dollar breath. Information is not the answer.

The kids, said Raspberry, all know about the former sports heroes who squandered their fortunes and futures for a high higher than the last high. And yet they rush into the streets to plunge into their own drug habit. "What is it about people," Raspberry asks, "that makes them take such overwhelming risks for such trivial pleasure? Ignorance isn't the problem. Stupidity compounded with arrogance is, and drug education, no matter how well-intended, can't cure that." Most Christians agree.

Finally, Christians join Gerald Grant in questioning whether education can function without authority. In our therapeutic culture many Americans are deeply suspicious of authority. The term provokes fears of mind control and all those visions of Orwell's *1984*. These fears are often fed by the confusion of authority with authoritarianism. But they are markedly different things.

Authority is essentially impersonal; it belongs to the collective tradition. Authoritarianism, by contrast, is essentially an expression of personal will. If a policeman says, "The law prohibits you from parking here," I ought to listen to him out of deference to authority. But if a resident says, "Don't park in front of my house. I won't allow it," I have reason to suspect nothing more than an authoritarian spirit.

In any healthy society it is authority that saves us from authoritarianism. The respect for the vital standards of the law, culture, and religion delivers us from the countless petty authoritarian voices and assertive egos. Society depends upon motorists who respect the authority of the policeman, writers who respect the authority of the dictionary, and students who respect the authority of teachers.[13]

While many thoughtful Americans recognize the need for authority in our kind of world, Christians defend its values because they have already encountered the ultimate Authority in the "good news" of Jesus Christ. The gospel lays claim to our loyalties, not out of any arbitrary authoritarianism, but out of the authority of truth. That is why Christians recognize the value of authority in education. Truth, they contend, often comes through the voice of authority.

Options Before Christians

What are the alternatives for those Christian parents concerned about the demise of traditional values in America's schools? Judged by current responses of parents, five options lie before them.

First, they can join with other concerned citizens to press for the reform of public schools. Today's reformers are divided into two camps. One camp calls for a core curriculum, for raising the levels of competence of schoolteachers, and for greater emphasis on communication skills. The other camp considers the school an extension of the home and insists that schools teach the values of the parents. Some evangelical Christians support the first camp, but the vast majority of them stand with the second group and the call for a return to moral standards and teaching authority. That is the significance of the political effort to restore a nondenominational prayer, or at least a moment of silence, to the daily program.

Second, concerned Christians can move to the suburbs where parents seem to exercise more influence over the values and goals of public schools. Many Christians have already exercised this option and have found most of the same problems in sub-urban schools.

Third, Christian parents can follow the lead of many Asian parents with children in metropolitan school districts and maintain close-knit family ties within an "immigrant ethic." The strong family ties and high expectations of Asian parents are now widely regarded as basic factors in the superior schoolwork of Asian children even in American urban public schools. Christian families, immigrants of another sort, could recover their own emphasis on family unity and values as means of resisting the negative influences on today's schoolyard.

Fourth, they can offer home instruction for their children. An increasing number of parents are opting for this alternative. In 1975 an estimated 10,000 children were being taught at home. By 1986 that figure had grown to 160,000. Today only a handful of states fail to grant official recognition to home instruction.

Fifth, concerned parents can send their children to a private Christian school. In spite of the added costs for education, millions of Christians, as we have seen, are choosing this option.[14]

Whatever course of action Christian parents choose, they have one primary responsibility in American culture: to convince their children and their neighbors that their criticism of American public schools does not spring from less loyalty to America but more.

Back in 1785 the legislature of Georgia chartered the first state university in the United States. The preamble of the act affirmed:

> Among the first objects of those who wish well to national prosperity, [are] to encourage and support the principles of religion and morality, and early to place the youth under the forming hand of society, that by instruction they may be moulded to the love of virtue and good.[15]

That is the spirit that must motivate exiled Christians in a democracy, an insistence upon morality in public education that springs from our love for "national prosperity."

FURTHER READING

Allan Bloom, *The Closing of the American Mind* (1987)

Gerald Grant, *The World We Created at Hamilton High 1953-1987* (1987)

Patricia M. Lines, "The New Private Schools and Their Historic Purpose," *Phi Delta Kappan*, January 1986, 373-79.

David Tyack and Elisabeth Hansot, *Managers of Virtue: Public School Leadership in America, 1820-1980* (1982)

Chapter 7, Notes

1. Gerald Grant, *The World We Created at Hamilton High 1953-1987* (Cambridge, Mass.: Harvard University Press, 1987), 54.

2. Ibid., 56-57. In *Managers of Virtue: Public School Leadership in America, 1820-1980* (New York: Basic Books, 1982), David Tyack and Elisabeth Hansot describe the dramatic changes since 1960 as an "attack" upon the governance of educational experts.

"Traditional leaders," they write, "have been assaulted by dispossessed groups and deligitimized by competing elites. Educational policy making has become politicized and fragmented. Beginning with blacks and their white allies in the civil-rights campaign, successive groups—feminists, Hispanics, the handicapped, native Americans, and many others—have mounted powerful protest movements to win practical and symbolic gains. . . . Many factions have found the law a ready instrument of challenge and reform, and, as a result, a new kind and degree of litigiousness has emerged. . . ."

As a consequence, leaders have lost the ability to command respect "either as aristocrats of character or as experts" and people have come to wonder if anyone is in charge (p. 8).

3. See Grant, *Hamilton High*, 184-85.

4. See ibid., 186-87.

5. See Tyack and Hansot, *Managers of Virtue*, 39.

6. See Henry Steele Commager, *The American Mind* (New Haven, Conn.: Yale University Press, 1950), 35.

7. Ibid., 38-39.

8. Quoted in Alice Felt Tyler, *Freedom's Ferment* (New York: Harper & Row, 1962), 234.

9. See Lyle E. Schaller, *It's a Different World* (Nashville: Abingdon Press, 1987), 103-6. Between *Abington Township v. Schempp* in 1963 and *Stone v. Graham* in 1980, the Supreme Court developed a three-part test for establishment clause cases. This test was applied in *Stone v. Graham* to a Kentucky law requiring that the Ten Commandments be posted in every public school classroom. The opinion of the Court read:

> This Court has announced a three-part test for determining whether a challenged state statute is permissible under the Establishment Clause of the United States Constitution:
> First, the statute must have a secular legislative purpose; second, its principal or primary effect must be one that neither advances nor inhibits religion; . . . finally the statute must not foster "an excessive government entanglement with religion."
> If a statute violates any of these three principles, it must be struck down under the Establishment Clause. We conclude that Kentucky's statute requiring the posting of the Ten Commandments in public school-rooms had no secular legislative purpose, and is therefore unconstitutional. (See John F. Wilson and Donald L. Drakeman, eds., *Church and State in American History* [Boston: Beacon Press, 1987], 236.)

10. See Patricia M. Lines, "The New Private Schools and Their Historic Purpose," *Phi Delta Kappan*, January 1986, 373-79.

11. Quoted in James Hitchcock, *What Is Secular Humanism?* (Ann Arbor, Mich.: Servant Books, 1982), 66.

12. Charles Colson, *Kingdoms in Conflict* (Grand Rapids: Zondervan Publishing House, 1987), 213.

13. See Harry Blamires, *Where Do We Stand?* (Ann Arbor, Mich.: Servant Books, 1980), 69-74.

14. See Schaller, *Different World*, 106-7.

15. Quoted in ibid., 116.

PART 3

PRIVATE DREAMS

In this part of our study we want to look at four representative areas of the American's private life, areas where many Christians struggle with biblical standards and cultural influence. These are four common elements of the American Dream, four ideals in our private lives: success, work, family, and love. In each case, while Christians encounter tensions with contemporary American values, they can, with God's help, demonstrate for their relatives and neighbors an alternative way of life arising from the gospel.

Chapter Eight
The Ladder to Success

"A high standard of living, in our post-ascetic culture, is considered the permitting condition for attaining a higher quality of life."
—Philip Rieff, in *The Triumph of the Therapeutic*

Shawn Clarkson always saw himself as a winner. He liked to tell people that by the time he was thirty-five, he was going to be a millionaire. "My business is exploding! It's going off like fireworks," he would say.

A lanky six-footer with curly brown hair and a slightly rumpled appearance, Clarkson was a "super-nice guy" with an appealing sense of humor. He was bright, thoughtful, and generous almost to a fault.

By 1984, with three years to go to make his million, he had acquired many of the outward symbols of success. He was flying to Dallas from his home in Phoenix on business once a week. He drove a company car. He had just moved his wife and two children into a fashionable four-bedroom house with a vaulted ceiling and a spiral staircase.

Shawn had spent two years as program chairman for the local Lions Club, and had served as president of the two-hundred-member Arizona chapter of the American Institute of Chemical Engineers. He was a thirty-second-degree Mason, and a board member for the Boys Club.

Ambitious and determined, an aggressive go-getter, Clarkson was considered by his friends as "extremely goal-oriented." He was a young man on the move, a good promoter, a talented salesman, a smooth talker.

Prominently displayed on Shawn's desk in his office was a bronze medallion with an image of the Statue of Liberty on one side and an American eagle on the other. He made a point of telling visitors he thought of himself not as the statue, with its feet embedded in solid concrete, but as the eagle, free as the wind and able to go wherever he wanted in life.

But behind all his talk, Shawn was losing control of his life. In a frenzy of activity, he was wheeling and dealing in areas beyond his expertise and falling behind in his consulting work. Then on a Sunday in May 1985, the family missed church for the first time in months. Shawn spent the day struggling in vain to scrape together enough cash to salvage his business, his image, and his pride.

About 11:30 that night, with the rest of his family in bed, several drinks under his belt, a handful of insurance policies all laid out neatly on the coffee table, and sixty cigarette butts in the ash trays, Shawn Clarkson walked barefooted into his garage, got into his BMW, and turned on the ignition. Within minutes he was dead from the poisonous exhaust fumes.

While I have changed the names, dates, and places in the story to avoid any embarrassment for family or friends, Shawn's story is real. Something like it happens almost every week in some major city in America. Why? Because so many Americans are in breathless pursuit of the Dream called "success." They really believe that "you can have it all." Comfort, status, power.

The Bible, however, presents a strikingly different vision of prosperity. At the heart of success in the biblical tradition is the Lord God and the special needs that human beings have because they are created in his likeness. We all have a soul, and we will never find our Dream of success if we deny or ignore this fundamental fact of our human nature.

The American Way to Success

In an earlier day, as we have seen, the American Dream stood for visions of a civil, just, religious, and generous American community. Katharine Lee Bates caught the vision in her lines:

America! America! May God thy gold refine,
Till all success be nobleness,
And ev'ry gain divine!

Some Americans still think that such a world is possible, but in recent years the American Dream more often stands for certain symbols of personal prosperity. Today the magnetic "good life," out there in the future, includes a four-bedroom house in suburbia, at least two late-model cars, four weeks of vacation, the toys to go with it, and an income adequate for the payments. The happiness Americans crave is supposed to come with an independent life-style that allows us to do what we really want to do. Freedom and fulfillment come somewhere toward the top of the ladder to success.

This American Dream called "success," then, blends elements from the two recent strands of American culture, the economic and the therapeutic. It is the predominant Dream of the middle class.

That interesting expression—"the middle class"— once stood for "middling interests" or "middling conditions" between poverty and wealth. But in the closing decades of the nineteenth century the term came to stand for people on the rise who were "calculating" and "ambitious." So American culture depicted the middle class more and more as those rising indefinitely to new levels of affluence and progress. And in this sense it came to include almost everyone in America.[1]

Most Americans know that the steps toward the top are not easy, but they are convinced that the rewards of success are well worth the cost. So they shape their lives, public and private, to achieve their Dream of the good life. The mother enters the work force, infants enter day-care centers, and the whole family enters into debt.

For several decades now the ladder has been a symbol of this middle-class success. Anyone who has bought a stepladder lately, however, knows that today's ladders are covered with warning labels. Apparently a multitude of lawsuits, filed by people who were careless with ladders, have forced manufacturers to warn: "When climbing this ladder, look out for the crash!"

The warning is good, not only for ladders but for life in America's money culture. Shawn Clarkson could have used one. Christians above all people should know that the gospel of the Lord Jesus Christ has a strikingly different description of the human condition and what it takes to make men and women genuinely prosperous. What, after all, is life? And can "the lifestyle of the rich and famous" deliver it?

This contemporary encounter of Christian values and American culture was described in some detail a century ago in an unexpected source, the novel *The Brothers Karamazov*, written by the great Russian novelist Fyodor Dostoevsky. The novel contains an episode called "The Grand Inquisitor" which sets forth Dostoevsky's penetrating meditation on the meaning of spiritual freedom.

Through a series of trips to Western Europe and the writings of Russian radicals, Dostoevsky had encountered the nineteenth-century liberal gospel of human progress and the notion of man's perfectibility based on his practical achievements. It was a faith that most Americans have come to share. Dostoevsky, however, was staunchly opposed to it because he knew that the Bible's picture of human nature was far more realistic.

The story of "The Grand Inquisitor" comes in the midst of a gripping dialogue between two of the Karamazov brothers, Alyosha, a Christian, and Ivan, an atheist. As they sit together in a restaurant, soon to be separated for years, Alyosha makes clear his longing for his brother to come to faith in Christ. Ivan, however, tells Alyosha that he cannot believe in God because the heart-rending suffering of innocent children makes belief in God impossible. To illustrate his unbelief, Ivan tells an imaginary story of Christ's appearance on earth in Seville at the height of the Spanish Inquisition.

Ivan relates that while Christ is ministering to suffering people outside the Seville cathedral, he is suddenly seized by the Inquisitor's guards and thrown into a gloomy dungeon. There, in the dark of night, an old Cardinal, the Grand Inquisitor, appears to interrogate Jesus and to describe to him what it is about human beings that explains their eagerness to surrender their lives to enslaving dreams of happiness.

The Inquisitor focuses upon Jesus' temptation in the wilderness and the ways he misjudged human nature in his encounter with the Evil One. "We succeed in ruling over men on earth," said the old Cardinal, "because we appeal to human weaknesses. We give them bread instead of freedom, miracles instead of true faith, and temporal power to maintain our spiritual authority."[2]

Through the argument of the old, withered Cardinal and the silence of Christ, Dostoevsky dramatizes the fact that every person, including every American today, faces a profound choice. Is real life, fulfilling life, found in the attainment of comfort, status, and power? Or is life found in the spiritual freedom that Jesus promised?

Dostoevsky knew that Jesus offered people a special vision of prosperity. It was not success as most Americans describe it, any more than it was the dream of most progressive-minded nineteenth-century Russians. One rather obscure incident in Jesus' life makes this spotlessly clear. He was teaching in Galilee when a man stepped out of the crowd and asked Jesus to arbitrate a dispute over an inheritance. Jesus refused and responded to the man, "Watch out! Be on your guard against all kinds of greed; a man's life does not consist in the abundance of his possessions."

Life isn't found in possessions? Can we imagine a more revolutionary outlook for an American?

The dramatic demonstration of Jesus' world of inverted values, as the Grand Inquisitor knew so well, can be found in the temptation of Jesus in the wilderness. Here was the compelling test of moral conscience, the blow-by-blow account of the battle of beliefs over human nature and personal happiness.

The dramatic encounter, recorded in Matthew 4, suggests that Jesus himself drew aside the curtain on this spiritual struggle (He was apparently the only one there!) in order to expose the emptiness and futility of the search for success in comfort, status, and power. And it is that disclosure that makes the story a significant commentary on the encounter of the Christian gospel with American culture.

What Could Be More Natural?

According to the account, Jesus' first temptation was to turn the desert stones into loaves of bread. For days he had suffered the pangs of hunger. His weakened body cried out for nourishment. So what could be more natural than for him to eat? "God gave us appetites!" the Tempter implied. "Surely he plans for us to eat."

Isn't "bread" one of those fundamental passions of people? In Dostoevsky's story the Grand Inquisitor told Jesus, "Had You chosen 'bread,' You would have satisfied the universal and everlasting craving of human beings and of the individual to find someone to worship."

The temptation echoes today in the incessant appeal of America's therapeutic culture: "Don't worry. Be happy." Advertisers urge us to think of number one. "You deserve a break today." "Pamper yourself." It is the heartbeat of selfism. We all have, it says, these cravings for physical pleasures. Surely they are not meant to deceive us. Life must consist in the satisfaction of our deepest feelings.

We all know the argument. We have all heard our own inner thoughts: "You've worked hard for what you've got. Who is going to begrudge you a little pleasure. Besides, if it's natural, it must be right. Hunger is natural, so eat to your heart's content! Sex is natural, so why resist a beautiful, natural thing? How can God himself deny you what he has put within you?"

For at least a generation now, Americans by the millions have rushed to receive this feel-good "gospel." It is essentially the pursuit of happiness for the expressive individualist. "If you feel the strong urge to go to bed with someone else's husband or wife, why let some traditional taboo stand in your way?"

That is the point, why? What is wrong with enjoying life? Why should any person choose to say, "No"? Why did Jesus say, "No"?

The biblical story tells us. Jesus responded to the tempter's appeal, "People do not live by bread alone but by every word that comes from the mouth of God." He spotted this first, all-too-common misstep on the ladder to success: bread, the hunger for personal satisfaction. The One who "knew what was in man" recognized the half-truth in the temptation, and he underscored that side of life higher than the physical, a side only fools dare to neglect.

Human beings, Jesus said, do not live by bread alone. If we search for success while living like animals, satisfying only our physical hungers, we will never find life and no real, fulfilling success. The secret of being human is not only to live but to have something to live for. Any life that fails to come to terms with the hungers of the soul is self defeating. It can never lead to real success, because neither economic progress nor raw pleasure alone will ever nourish the human spirit.[3]

English novelist and critic G. K. Chesterton once said, "If I find a friend at the bar having his tenth whisky and soda and I want to convince him to stop, I slap him on the back and say, 'Be a man!' But no one who wanted to dissuade a crocodile from eating its tenth missionary would slap it on the back and say, 'Be a crocodile!' "[4]

We know when a person is living a subhuman kind of life. It is when she lives like an animal and tries to deny her own soul and its needs. If we respond to life like mere animals, true success is impossible.

What's the Popular Thing to Do?

The second temptation Jesus encountered suggested that he ought to jump from the heights of the great Jewish temple, apparently to confirm the teaching of the Jewish rabbis who expected the Messiah to show himself on the temple roof. Who wouldn't be impressed by such a miracle?

Since first-century Jews habitually looked for miraculous signs, here was a chance for Jesus to play to the gallery, to exhibit a marvelous trust in God's miraculous power and so gain a following by becoming a public sensation.

Which of us doesn't feel the seduction of the suggestion? Who isn't hypnotized by a trapeze artist or tightrope walker forty stories up? Here is the lure of the spectacular . . . the temptation of the crowd pleaser, the instant celebrity. This risk on the ladder to success is still with us, as Bellah and his team argue in *Habits of the Heart:*

For over a hundred years, a large part of the American people, the middle class, has imagined that the virtual meaning of life lies in the acquisition of ever-increasing status, income, and authority, from which genuine freedom is supposed to come. . . .

Some of us often feel, and most of us sometimes feel, that we are only someone if we have "made it" and can look down on those who have not. The American dream is often a very private dream of being the star, the uniquely successful and admirable one, the one who stands out from the crowd of ordinary folk who don't know how.[5]

Success, then, in American culture apparently means climbing higher than your competition so that people will be forced to look up to you. Status! That is the word for it. After all, who doesn't want to be admired and envied? That is why our American search for success often dictates the styles we wear, the cars we drive, and the friends we make. It can drag us into drugs and premature sex, in the misguided hope of making it with the right people. The temptation runs throughout American culture.

According to the gospel account, however, Jesus refused to surrender to the ever-so-subtle suggestion. He wanted followers who truly trusted him, not a crowd looking for spectacular entertainment. Dostoevsky's old Inquisitor recognized the intent when he said to Jesus, "You did not descend from the Cross when they shouted to You, mocking and reviling You, 'If thou be the Son of God, come down from the cross.' You did not descend, for again You would not enslave man by a miracle. You craved faith given freely, not based on a miracle. You craved for free love and not the base raptures of the slave before the might that has overawed him forever."[6]

Since Jesus saw through the temptation, he labeled it for what it really was—a test of God. He knew the Almighty was not going to be any man's debtor. No one can pull the right string and get God to jump because God is complete in himself. He is self-sufficient and too clean to be bribed or manipulated. That too is reality and an essential element in biblical faith and genuine success.

Air Force pilots of speedy fighter planes tell us how easy it is to get disoriented in a dogfight at twenty thousand feet. For that reason, after coming out of a spin, a well-trained pilot always tries to find a visual horison as soon as possible, some huge object outside his spinning airplane, such as a mountain range, to get reoriented to reality.

In the American pursuit of success it is just as easy to lose a sense of direction, to doubt God, and to rush madly after a wish-dream, the admiration of other people. Christians are not exempt from this dizziness, but they know, if they are Christian in more than name, that God's truth is a mountain peak. In a spinning world of private dreams, there is something to count on.

Isn't Winning Everything?

According to the gospel story, the tempter finally shoved aside his underhanded tricks and tried the no-nonsense, head-on approach. He offered Jesus the allegiance of the nations, the worship of believing masses, on one little condition: the acceptance of illegitimate power.

It was an example of that timeless temptation that says, "If it is God's will for you to gain a kingdom, then turn to the stuff of kingdoms: power." Translated into contemporary terms, the final temptation promises that prosperity is out there for anyone willing to bend the rules in order to gain it. Wasn't it the fabulously wealthy Daddy Warbucks in *Annie* who said, "It doesn't matter who you step on, on the way to the top, if you don't plan to come back down"?

In America's economic culture it is all too easy to

say, "We all have to make a living the best way we can. Everybody has to cut a few corners here and there. What's wrong with stretching the truth in an ad or slipping a little cash under the table? It's just a way of doing business. Everybody does it. How else are you going to keep a step ahead of the competition?"

What is wrong? The wrong is written across the lives of those who have fallen in the race to the top. Life on an escalator is anything but comfortable. The American Dream called "success" demands ambition, the ability to respond to rapidly changing conditions, and the willingness to leave family and home to follow some opportunity for advancement in a career. Success in today's America leaves no room for that old-fashioned sense of fulfillment that comes in setting aside competition and in giving oneself in the service of others.

After twenty years counseling the rich and the famous in the New York City area, Thomas Pike wrote, "The temporary fame, power, or financial benefits of the Success Cult may be seductive, but the ultimate end is always dissatisfaction, personal difficulties, and sometimes outright disaster. Some of the classic signs that the American Success Cult has thoroughly ravaged a person's life include a broken marriage, damaged health, a radical realization that one's life lacks ultimate meaning, or even sudden death."[7]

As early as the 1830s Tocqueville noted the American's restlessness in the midst of prosperity. "In America," he said, "I have seen the freest and best educated of men in circumstances the happiest to be found in the world; yet it seemed to me that a cloud habitually hung on the brow, and they seemed serious and almost sad even in their pleasures," because they "never stop thinking of the good things they have not got."[8]

Have times really changed? Contemporary American culture, like the tempter in the wilderness, offers hungry people a dream world. "Success is more things, a busier life, making it with the right people."

But we must remember Shawn Clarkson. Do we really expect to find life without pain, happiness without discipline, or success without the cross? The Bible offers us no such hope. It teaches us instead that there can be no genuine prosperity without Christ, without repentance, and without faith. God has made us with yearnings of eternity in our hearts, and any genuine success must always rest upon this fundamental fact of the human condition.

FURTHER READING

Robert N. Bellah and others, *Habits of the Heart* (1985)
Fyodor Dostoevsky, *Notes from the Underground and the Grand Inquisitor*, trans. Ralph E. Matlaw (1960)
Thomas Pike and William Proctor, *Is It Success? Or Is It Addiction?* (1988)

Chapter 8, Notes

1. See Robert N. Bellah and others, *Habits of the Heart* (New York: Harper & Row, 1985), 119-20.
2. Fyodor Dostoevsky, *Notes from the Underground and the Grand Inquisitor*, trans. Ralph E. Matlaw (New York: E. P. Dutton, 1960).
3. In arguing that modernity's vision has failed, T. J. Jackson Lears writes: "The Grand Inquisitor is no longer a withered churchman but a sleek corporate or government executive who rehabilitates the 'anti-social,' entertains the restless, and feeds the hungry—but only some of them, some of the time. The new subtler rationalization of twentieth-century culture has not suppressed the continuing irrationalities of the business cycle. Even in the affluent West, economic security remains problematic except for the well-to-do minority. And . . . psychic fulfillment, though it has become an obsessive goal, seems equally elusive for all classes. The denial of sin, the abandonment of moral responsibility, the sacrifice of freedom—nothing has brought the happiness promised by prophets of modernity." (*No Place of Grace: Antimodernism and the Transformation of American Culture 1880-1920* [New York: Pantheon Books, 1981], 300.)
4. Quoted in Stuart Barton Babbage, *Man in Nature and in Grace* (Grand Rapids: Wm. B. Eerdmans Publishing Co., 1957), 9.
5. Bellah, *Habits of the Heart*, 284-85.
6. Dostoevsky, *Notes from the Underground*, 130-31.
7. Thomas Pike and William Proctor, *Is It Success? Or Is It Addiction?* (Nashville: Thomas Nelson Publishers, 1988), 29.
8. Quoted in Bellah, *Habits of the Heart*, 117.

Chapter Nine
Thank God It's Friday

"Most of us, like the assembly line worker, have jobs that are too small for our spirit. Jobs are not big enough for people."

—Nora Watson, staff writer for a health care publisher

*I*n April 1988 national news wires carried the story of the death of a self-educated janitor named Lawrence Hummel, who wore his lawyer's hand-me-downs but who left over $600,000 to Bethany College in northern West Virginia, where he mopped floors for thirty years. Based on his knowledge of the stock market gleaned from discussions with professors and from economics classes at the college, Hummel had amassed a million-dollar fortune. But to the end of his life he continued to live frugally.

"If you saw him and talked with him," said Joseph Gompers, his lawyer, "you might confuse him with a bum. But he wasn't. He was a warm, compassionate person who cared about people."[1]

The story made news, no doubt, because Lawrence Hummel, according to the standards of contemporary American culture, was a misfit. He saw no need to turn his wealth into any of the normally accepted symbols of the American Dream: clothes, travel, homes, or cars. Work, for Mr. Hummel, had a higher purpose. Thoughtful Christians have always claimed the same thing.

Why Work?

Why do we work? That is one of those questions that reveals the invisible cultural forces that shape our lives. One answer, probably the prevailing one in America today, comes from contemporary culture. Another one comes from the biblical tradition.

In the economic version of the American Dream the answer to the question, "Why work?" is traceable to Adam Smith's classic treatise *The Wealth of Nations*. In 1776 the Scottish professor of moral philosophy argued that people work because it is in their own enlightened self-interest. "Every individual," Smith wrote, "is continually exerting himself to find out the most advantageous employment for whatever capital he can command."

Capitalism, then, based on Adam Smith's view, harnesses our innate selfishness for the "common good." While governments are responsible for the protection of life and property, the hands of government should be kept off business and industry. The best interests of society will be served by allowing natural laws of supply and demand to operate unimpeded.

Capitalism in America has changed dramatically in the last two generations. Government hands now seem to be everywhere. Yet evidence of the creativity and productivity that the laissez-faire philosophy has fostered remains. We are surrounded with tangible promises of the American economic Dream: appliances, cars, conveniences, and toys of all shapes and sizes.

At the same time thoughtful observers of the American scene are acutely aware of the widespread addiction to self-interest, the passion for consumer products, and the empty spirit of today's American worker.

The work ethic of today's upwardly mobile American was characterized not long ago by a bit of humor in the *Washington Post*:

> Now I lay me down to sleep
> I pray my Cuisinart to keep
> I pray my stocks are on the rise
> And that my analyst is wise
> That all the wine I sip is white
> And that my hot tub's watertight
> That racquetball won't get too tough
> That all my sushi's fresh enough
> I pray my cordless phone still works
> That my career won't lose its perks
> My microwave won't radiate
> My condo won't depreciate
> I pray my health club doesn't close
> And that my money market grows
> If I go broke before I wake
> I pray my Volvo they won't take.[2]

A surprising number of Americans in quest of this economic Dream are growing restless in the workplace. One recent poll indicated that one out of four Americans is unhappy in his or her job. The reasons the workers most often gave for their unhappiness were the desires for greater recognition, more money, less stress, and a better boss.

This frustration in the workplace comes in large part because people feel the squeeze of two conflicting attitudes toward work. On the one hand, Americans are influenced by those dreams from our economic culture that portray the workplace as a source of happiness and personal fulfillment. Even when we are not sure how to define work, we know that it is linked somehow with a sense of self. What we *do* is supposed to describe what we *are*.

When an American meets someone for the first time, he will ask the predictable question, "What do you do?" The frequency of the question is a clue to the idolization of jobs in America. We assess a person's worth according to his employment. We are what we do, aren't we?

Back in the 1970s Studs Terkel wrote a hefty volume titled *Working* in which he let scores of workers describe their feelings about their jobs. Most of them nurtured the dream that they would somehow "find themselves" in their work. When some suddenly found themselves on the list of the unemployed, they were devastated.

Dr. John R. Coleman, president of Haverford College, probably expressed the trauma best. He had taken an unusual sabbatical in 1973 during which he worked at menial jobs. While working as a porter-dishwasher, he was fired.

"I'd never been fired," he recalled, "and I'd never been unemployed. For three days I walked the streets. Though I had a bank account, though my children's tuition was paid, though I had a salary and a job waiting for me back in Haverford, I was demoralized."[3]

Work and a sense of worth apparently do go together, at least for most Americans. It is easy for us to think of our jobs as the sure route to fulfillment and success. This attitude is but one short step removed from thinking of our job as our god. Many an executive or salesman or accountant forgets his family and has no time for religion or God—while he claws and scratches his way to the top.

On the other hand, recent years have convinced many Americans that work can never be satisfying in itself. Many of us endure work only so long as it promises a satisfactory private life. Work, more recent American culture would have us believe, is simply a necessary evil of physical existence, a mere means to personal pleasure.

These Americans live from one coffee break to

another or one weekend to the next. Work is the place to accumulate the cash for another escape to Maui or the Bahamas. So a job for these Americans is always a barrier to happiness—never a way of happiness. It is a mountain to climb in order to enjoy some picnic at the top, a dangerous trail to follow.

The futility of meaningless work was reflected in the thirty-seven-year-old steel worker, Mike Lefevre, who told Studs Terkel,

> I'm a dying breed. A laborer. Strictly muscle work. . . . It's hard to take pride in a bridge you're never gonna cross, in a door you're never gonna open. You're mass-producing things and you never see the end result of it.
>
> I would like to see a building, say, the Empire State, I would like to see on one side of it a foot-wide strip from top to bottom with the name of every bricklayer, the name of every electrician, with all the names. So when a guy walked by, he could take his son and say, "See, that's me over there on the fifty-fifth floor. I put the steel beam in." Picasso can point to a painting. What can I point to? A writer can point to a book. Everybody should have something to point to.[4]

Can't we also detect this note of futility in the popular way Americans refer to the approaching weekend? "TGIF," we say. "Thank God, it's Friday."

Can't we catch the same attitude in our TV commercials? A beer ad not long ago showed four friends in their fishing clothes, surrounded by a breathtaking mountain scene. They were sitting around a warm, glowing fire. The fish were in the skillet, and the beer was on ice. Everyone smiled as one of the men held up a chilled can and said, "It doesn't get any better than this."

The point is obvious: Life isn't found on the job accomplishing anything significant. It is found instead with the boys, outdoors, on a weekend with food and a special beer.

Hosts of Americans today have abandoned the traditional Puritan work ethic, and according to sociologist Daniel Bell, their capitalism survives but without the advantage of any moral or transcendent ethic. Justification of work today emphasizes "an extraordinary contradiction within the social structure itself. On the one hand, the business corporation wants an individual to work hard, pursue a career, accept delayed gratification—to be, in the crude sense, an organization man. And yet, in its products and its advertisements, the corporation promotes pleasure, instant joy, relaxing, and letting go. One is to be 'straight' by day and a 'swinger' by night. This is self-fulfillment and self-realization!"[5]

Work in the Bible

What is the Christian alternative to the raw self-interest of the recent American Dream? The Bible teaches that work is ordained of God for our human benefit.

During his years in prison Dostoevsky, the Russian novelist, discovered that if a prisoner "had to move a heap of earth from one place to another and back again—I believe the convict would hang himself ... preferring rather to die than endure . . . such humiliation, shame and torture." As a result of his experience, he later wrote that if you wanted to utterly crush a man, you only had to give him work of a completely irrational sort. Isn't that a fitting commentary on unbelief in our secular America? If we deny the existence of God, we are condemned to a senseless universe.[6]

That is the significance of the Christian view of work. In their book *Why Work?* John Bernbaum and Simon Steer summarize the biblical teaching in five basic principles.

First, *work is a God-ordained task for people*. According the Genesis story of creation, the command to work comes from One who is himself a worker.

Work was not a result of sinful rebellion; it was a part of God's original intention for human beings. According to Genesis, God commands humanity to "fill the earth and subdue it. Rule over the fish of the sea and the birds of the air and over every living creature."

Second, as a result of the Fall, the fundamental human rebellion against God, *work is no longer the fulfilling joy God intended it to be*. Human rebellion is reflected in human work. The biblical account of the human condition underscores two common abuses of work. It can become a means of exploitation or oppression, and it can become an idol.

The Teacher of Ecclesiastes is one striking example of our human frustration. "I built houses for myself," he writes, "and planted vineyards. I bought male and female slaves. I amassed silver and gold for myself. Yet when I surveyed all that my hands had done . . . everything was meaningless, a chasing after the wind."

Third, *Jesus Christ has redeemed our work from the curse*. The fact that the incarnate God worked at a carpenter's bench is a striking testimony to the sanctity of the workplace. When Christ is there, as we shall see, work assumes a new significance.

Fourth, *work, for the Christian, is to be done as a service to Christ*. "Slaves," wrote the apostle Paul, "whatever you do, work at it with all your heart, as working for the Lord, not for men, since you know that you will receive an inheritance from the Lord as a reward. It is the Lord Christ you are serving."

Finally, the Bible tells us that *work not only brings glory to God if done for him, but it has moral benefits as well*. In 2 Thessalonians 3:6-13, the apostle tells us that we should work in order to provide for ourselves and our families. And in Ephesians 4:28 he urges believers to undertake work that is useful, that we may have "something to share with those in need."[7]

Is there any chance that the Christian view of work can help to renew today's workplace? It can, in two fundamental ways: in the view of life that Christians communicate in their work and in the quality of the work they do for others.

Certain vocations influence the thinking and viewpoints of people in a special way. The public has come to expect those involved in these vocations to address the questions of the mind. It goes, as we say, with the territory. All those positions that directly or indirectly address the questions of life and its meaning fall into this category: teachers, scriptwriters, politicians, psychologists, advertisers, editors, social workers, judges, artists, and many others.

Since Christians hold a special view about the kind of creatures we are and what is in store for us in the future, Christians in these "meaning-of-life" vocations carry a special responsibility. They must reflect the Christian view of people, the Christian way of life, and the Christian convictions regarding human destiny. And when they reflect these beliefs, they will make a difference in American life.

In many other vocations the questions of ultimate purpose and human destiny never affect the quality of the work itself. A plumber's work, for example, never addresses the question of life's meaning. The work may be done well without any direct reference to Christian truth and values. In this sense, there is no such thing as Christian plumbing.

In these sorts of vocations, the Christian reflects his faith by the quality of his work. Being a Christian affects the plumber's work in that he works honestly and does the best work he can. Serious-minded Christians, then, in all sorts of vocations—other than criminal and immoral ones—can bring to their work a new dignity, a new responsibility, and a new excellence.[8]

The Carpenter

Christians have always found significance in the fact that, before he became a quiet revolutionary rabbi, Jesus was a working man, a carpenter. Just how, then, does Jesus redeem our work?

We know little about Jesus from his birth to his baptism. But the fact that he worked with his hands for twenty years says something about Christianity and the workweek. It says we can all work with dignity. We do not have to withdraw from normal life in order to meet God.

In an earlier day Americans believed that. Honest labor was a way of making something of yourself. Work wasn't merely a way to make money but a means of making a living.

Our word *vocation* goes back to those colonial Puritans who shaped so much of our thinking about work. The word carries the thought that our work is a calling from God. The Lord himself, it implies, has a purpose for every person's work, whether as a nurse, a pilot, a lawyer, a mechanic, or, as Jesus, a carpenter. Work in the sight of God lifts labor out of the restrictions of the profit motive and lends it dignity.

Sometimes we forget how unusual Christianity is in this respect. Eastern religions encourage withdrawal from normal life in order to find God. Hinduism, Buddhism, and the so-called New Age religions insist that we must withdraw from the world for some special meditation led by some guru in order to find genuine spiritual life.

Not Christianity. The Bible never insists that we divorce worship and work. We need special times of worship, not to escape from anything but to be renewed to live and work for God in the world.

Jesus is himself the strongest argument for this. He was no junior guru with tender features of youth. When he extended his hands inviting those who labor to find rest in him, his palms were calloused and nicked—like the hands of every carpenter I have ever known.

And to the dignity of work Jesus added the value of responsibility. Jesus' hometown folks had watched him for thirty years. They had seen him grow up, had noticed his apprenticeship under Joseph, and when

Joseph died, they saw him assume the heavy responsibility for the family—his mother, his younger brothers and sisters. His hands had put food on the table and clothes on their backs.

When he left Nazareth to meet his cousin, John the Baptizer, at the Jordan River, it was no youthful religious zealot who accepted John's call for revival and baptism. It was a responsible carpenter who had demonstrated that work was not the road to personal success so much as the route to responsibility for others.

In our time it is almost impossible for Americans to see how their work serves the community at large. The growth of cities and the organization of labor have "privatized" work. In the last two generations, Americans have come to look upon their work almost exclusively from the perspective of personal advantages. Any benefit for the community—beyond economic growth—has largely dropped from view.

Christians, however, are governed by a higher conception of work. In the collect for Labor Day, the Episcopal *Book of Common Prayer* entreats God, "So guide us in the work we do, that we may do it not for self alone, but for the common good." It is that concern for the common good that lifts work out of the strictly private.

"The entrepreneur who creates hundreds of new jobs," says Denver's Archbishop J. Francis Stafford, "is performing a morally good act: he or she is giving fellow human beings an opportunity to exercise their capacity for honest work. Workers who perform their duties conscientiously and well, and trade unions which bargain in good faith for the rights of workers, are also moral agents, contributing to the integrity of the workplace."[9]

Quality Is Job One

Finally, Jesus' workbench suggests to us something about the quality of our daily work. Who, after all, can imagine Jesus turning out shoddy work? In

small towns like Nazareth there were village crafts-
men, handymen who with the simplest tools could
repair a gate, build useful cabinets, or make a table
and chairs. That's what Jesus was—a village crafts-
man in Nazareth. And his work for men was a reflection of his walk with God. The drawers of the cabinets
ran smoothly, the yokes were well balanced, the boxes
were square, and the toys were sturdy and safe.

Why does that sound like "the good old days"?
Has quality slipped from the American workplace?

Addison H. Leitch, the late Presbyterian professor at Gordon-Conwell Seminary, wrote not long
before he died about a time he made himself unpopular at a college convocation just before everyone
headed home for the holidays. "Suppose," Leitch said,
"that the last man to check out the jet plane on which
you will fly home did his job just as faithfully as you
have done yours here during the last semester."

A groan went up. The students knew they had
not always done their work as faithfully as they should
have. How could they be assured the airline maintenance man had performed his duties well? In a day of
restaurants that can't pass health inspections, air-
planes that fail safety checks, TV repairmen who don't
fix it, plumbers who don't show, police who take
bribes, engineers who steal calculators, and students
who lift books from libraries, how could they know the
maintenance man would do his job?

Quality is a Christian concern because the dedicated Christian knows that the daily job, in the office
or in the shop, can be an offering to God. It is never a
mere matter of personal choice.

Americans are trying to conduct business, run
companies, and get ahead today without any generally
accepted standards of right and wrong. Morality, we
like to think, is a matter of personal choice. "The business of America is business." But moral values are still
an important part of the workplace, and thoughtful
Christians are eager to explain how Christian commitment makes a difference in employers and employees.

Like Lawrence Hummel, they have an unusual view of work. They hold that the gospel brings dignity, responsibility, and quality to labor. Jesus Christ their Savior was, after all, a carpenter.

FURTHER READING

Daniel Bell, *The Cultural Contradictions of Capitalism* (1976)

John A. Bernbaum and Simon M. Steer, *Why Work?* (1986)

Connecticut Mutual Life Report on American Values in the '80s: The Impact of Belief (1981)

Leland Ryken, *Work and Leisure in Christian Perspective* (1987)

Chapter 9, Notes

1. *The Denver Post*, 20 April 1988.
2. Quoted in John A. Bernbaum and Simon M. Steer, *Why Work?* (Grand Rapids: Baker Book House, 1986), 44-45.
3. Studs Terkel, *Working* (New York: Pantheon Books, 1974), xvii-xviii.
4. Ibid., xxxi-xxxii.
5. Daniel Bell, *The Cultural Contradictions of Capitalism* (New York: Basic Books, 1976), 71-72.
6. Quoted in Joseph Frank, *Dostoevsky: Years of Ordeal* (Princeton, N.J.: Princeton University Press, 1983), 159.
7. See Bernbaum and Steer, *Why Work?*, 3-4.
8. The *Connecticut Mutual Report on American Values in the '80s* (Hartford, Conn.: Connecticut Mutual Life Insurance Co., 1981) revealed that "religion is a much greater predictor of work satisfaction than either income level or occupational status." The report also found that "those who are most committed to religion are substantially more positive about their work than the least religious" (pp. 164, 162).
9. J. Francis Stafford, "This Home of Freedom: A Pastoral Letter to the Church of Denver," 28 May 1987, 30.

Chapter Ten

Learning to Live without Others

"There's a lack of family cohesion now, a product of the celebration of the individual. As a result, we're almost like strangers living in the same household."[1]

—Dr. Greer Litton Fox, Director
Wayne State University's Family Resource Center
(1980)

*J*udy Blume's children's book *Superfudge* features a five-year-old boy, Fudge, who is seen through the eyes of his older brother, Peter. At Christmastime, Fudge makes a fuss over writing to Santa Claus by insisting that every member of the family write to the old gent. Peter must also write a letter for the baby sister and family dog. Peter privately complains to his mother and suggests it is about time they reveal the truth to Fudge. "After all," says Peter, "you told him where babies come from. How can a kid who knows where babies come from still believe in Santa?"

Fudge's mother, however, rejects Peter's argument and claims that knowing where babies come

143

from has nothing to do with belief in Santa. And, in any case, she says, "He's so enthusiastic and the idea of Santa is so lovely that Daddy and I have decided it can't possibly hurt." The parents find Fudge's belief cute and see his childhood innocence as a refreshing thing.

After all the letters to Santa get written, and after Fudge receives the shiny red bicycle he requested from Santa, Fudge confesses to his brother that he really knows there is no Santa, and that he has always known there is no Santa, but "because Mommy and Daddy think I believe in him . . . I pretend. . . . Aren't I a great pretender?"

Superfudge is a striking example of contemporary American families because it recognizes that the traditional roles of family members have been turned upside-down. Fudge puts on an act to make his parents happy. Though only five years old, he is so aware of the structure of adult-child relations that he can pretend to be unaware. He keeps his parents in ignorance of his access to information, turning adult-child relations on their head. The parents are more innocent than the children.[2]

Christians in America have always felt that the home is the indispensable environment for growing up and that parents are the essential interpreters of adulthood for children. The Bible itself seems to point in this direction when it commands: "Honor your father and your mother, so that you may live long in the land the Lord your God is giving you." For centuries this is what Christians and Jews have taught and tried to live.

Today, however, nowhere is the conflict greater between biblical religion and contemporary American culture than in the life of the family. In most families the American Dream comes to each member independently. It is not a family experience. As a result, many Christians, along with other Americans, are paying an enormous price for their higher standard of living, their personal "rights," and their neglect of family unity. They have surrendered control of their homes as the center of moral nurture to hostile social forces determined to destroy the American family.

Growing Up in America

Childhood in America is a preparation for that rite of passage to adulthood we call "leaving home." Almost from day one American parents launch their children on a lifelong search for the true self. They expect Jimmy and Sally to become self-reliant individuals capable of maneuvering through the rite of passage successfully. In the words of Robert Bellah, this transition is "a kind of second birth in which we give birth to ourselves." We are forced to find ourselves by leaving home, never to return again in the same sense.[3]

With this passage in view, American parents encourage their child from the earliest age to decide for himself, to make up her own mind. Almost as soon as children can process words, they hear, "Chocolate, strawberry, or vanilla?" Life in America is, after all, a giant candy store filled with limitless choices. Sally is encouraged to believe she is the best judge of what she wants and what she should do, and Jimmy comes to believe that he should have his own opinions and solve his own problems. He comes to think of his inner self as the source and standard for all values. What he likes is good; what he dislikes is bad. As a result American children, in comparison with children in other cultures, are marked by an intense self-centeredness.[4]

If the training works, sometime during his teen years Jimmy will determine "what he wants to be" and settle all the basic questions in life about reality and the path to happiness: "What career shall I pursue? Whom should I marry? Should religion have any place in my life?"

Even in those instances where the young American cannot decide for himself, he still prizes the illusion that he is the center of decision-making. When he needs to consult a banker, teacher, counselor, or expert of any kind, he considers it a gathering of information to help him make up his own mind. The expert is only a resource person, never a decision-maker.

The irony, says Bellah, is that just where we Americans think we are most free, we are most coerced by the dominant beliefs of our culture. "For it is a powerful cultural fiction that we not only can, but must, make up our deepest beliefs in the isolation of our private selves."[5]

The Family in Crisis

How are we coerced by our culture? The American family, as nearly everyone should know, is in crisis. The traditional spirit of independency—today under enormous stress created by new social forces—has brought hosts of American families to the breaking point. Daniel Patrick Moynihan, in his *Family and Nation*, has told the heart-breaking story and the frustrations of national policies over the past twenty-five years.

In major sectors of the inner city the traditional family—father, mother, and children—has almost disappeared. More than 50 percent of the children are born out of wedlock. And in the nation as a whole three in five children born today will live with a single parent by the time they reach age eighteen, a tragic statistic, not the tolerable condition the media lead us to believe.[6]

Separation and divorce have become so widespread that many treat them as commonplace experiences. They are not "ho-hum" experiences, however, for the children caught in them. Between 1970 and 1979 the number of teenagers affected by divorce and separation more than doubled. Some experts estimate that one million young people each year experience divorce and separation in their family.

This high incidence of divorce and separation means that many teenagers are in flux just when they are trying to discover who they really are. Parents wounded by their divorces often demand that their children suddenly condone behavior in their parents that was not approved in the household prior to the divorce. Since teen years, with their normal explorations of personal relationships, are tough enough, most teens cannot cope with the added emotional burden of immature parents who consume the time and understanding that teenagers themselves need.

The impact of separation and divorce upon the traditional family is compounded by the spreading epidemic of teenage mothers. By the late 1980s, according to the Alan Guttmacher Institute, one million American teenage girls become pregnant each year. Of that number 400,000 obtain abortions, 470,000 give birth, and the others miscarry. About half of those who give birth are under eighteen. "Nobody cares anymore whether or not you're a virgin," said fifteen-year-old Denisse Rosario, a volunteer counselor at one of the Planned Parenthood Federation's programs for adolescents in the South Bronx.[7]

While experts disagree over the causes of these staggering statistics, they reach almost complete consensus about the outcome: premature parenthood has negative effects upon mother, child, and family. Teenage mothers sixteen or younger are more likely than mothers in their early twenties to have babies with low birth weights. Low birth weight is, in turn, associated with many lifelong disabilities such as mental retardation, deafness, and blindness. These risks to the infant increase when the mother fails to receive proper prenatal care, and this is more likely if the girl is poor, nonwhite, and unmarried.

Teenage mothers frequently drop out of school; once out, they seldom return. With few job skills and an infant to care for, many teenage mothers are unable to find a job that pays more than they can receive from welfare. They are trapped in a web of circumstances that make it almost impossible to attain the sense of self and the standard of living they might have reached had they never become pregnant.[8]

David Elkind, professor of Child Study at Tufts University, concludes: "To be in the place of a parent while still being, in many respects, a child, to be in the place of nurturing when one's own needs for nurture are still strong, makes formation of a consistent, whole, and meaningful definition of self difficult if not impossible to attain."

Unfortunately the social conditions that give rise to teenage pregnancy are not easily remedied. This is particularly true today when the traditional restraints upon teenage sexual experimentation are missing and encouragement for engaging in sexual activity is present everywhere. Sex education is not the answer as long as every other avenue of information geared to the teenager—books, movies, television, music lyrics, advertising—proclaim the "joy of sex."[9]

Loss of Parental Authority

While the Bible assumes that parents will be the primary influence upon their children, forces in modern American society make it more and more difficult for children and parents to form strong psychological bonds. Agencies of socialized parenting have invaded our families and subtly altered the quality of the parent-child relationship. The authorities who shape today's culture and our personal values are the celebrities, scriptwriters, corporate executives, and social experts.[10]

Joshua Meyrowitz paints a striking picture of television's impact upon the American family:

> Childhood as a protected and sheltered period of life has all but disappeared. Children today seem less "childlike." Children speak more like adults, dress more like adults, and behave more like adults than they used to. In fact, the reverse is also true. There are indications that many adults who

have come of age within the last twenty years continue to speak, dress, and act much like overgrown children. Certainly, all children and adults do not and cannot behave exactly alike, but there are many more similarities in behavior than in the past. The traditional dividing lines are gone.[11]

Recent years reveal a marked shift in adult psychological temperament. One way to view the attitudes of the "me generation" is to consider them as adult manifestations of the egocentrism traditionally associated with children. Surveys indicate that adults' sense of responsibility for children is shrinking. "There is a drop in the willingness of parents to sacrifice for children, and a sharp decline in the numbers of parents whose thoughts about the future include concerns about their children's aspirations. Americans now rank cars above children as aspects of a 'good life.' "[12]

In millions of cases American youngsters are raising themselves. They have been denied the sort of parental care that provides what Elkind calls "markers," those signs of progress toward maturity that we all need. Traditionally, these markers designated the social order that moved from childhood, through adolescence, to adulthood.

The most significant of these markers between childhood and adulthood is the authority of adults. But it is precisely this authority of parents and teachers—the two classes of adults with whom children have traditionally interacted the most—that recent changes in society have conspired to undermine. When these adults lose their claim to superior competence, wisdom, and authority, children lose an all-important marker of their place in the social order.[13]

How did such a thing happen? The American economy, the welfare system, pop psychology, and the child's rights movement have all had a hand in it. But the most pervasive contributor to the decline is television. In the United States there is at least one televi-

sion set, and often more, in every family in the country. Furthermore, unlike other countries, Americans
have television available twenty-four hours a day. It is
simply too pervasive for today's parents to monitor
effectively.

In his masterful study, *No Sense of Place*, Professor Meyrowitz argues that childhood was once a
period of innocence when children were protected
and shielded from certain kinds of information available to adults. In the past two decades, however, this
protection of children has vanished. Today they are
exposed to all sorts of information, much of it damaging.

Apparently American society no longer regards
childhood innocence as a positive thing. "The widespread use of television," says Meyrowitz, "is equiva-
lent to a broad social decision to allow young children
to be present at wars and funerals, courtships and
seductions, criminal plots and cocktail parties."

We can no longer hide behind our faint appeals
for family viewing time. It isn't there, and studies show
that millions of children would not choose to watch it
if it were. "There may be children's books and adult
books," says Meyrowitz, "yet there is no children's
television and adult television. In terms of what people
can and do watch, there is simply 'television.' "[14]

The hard fact is that scriptwriters, producers,
and network officials are exposing youngsters today
to every form of human vice and depravity "under the
mistaken assumption that this will somehow inure
them to evil and prepare them to live successful, if not
virtuous and honorable, lives. This assumption rests
on the mistaken belief that a bad experience is the
best preparation for a bad experience. In fact, just the
reverse is true: *a good experience is the best preparation for a bad experience.*"[15]

According to one study: "One third of all TV charac-
ters portrayed on the screen support themselves
either by fighting crime or by committing it. The firing
of handguns is so common that a typical night in front
of the set can perhaps best be compared to an evening

spent in a shooting gallery. . . . In TV's world, murders take place more frequently and crime occurs about ten times more often than in the real world."[16]

The loss of childhood innocence, however, is even more obvious in the sexual information now readily available to the young. Network television's steady stream is supplemented today by cable television and R-rated films available for home viewing. Taken together these mean that children at an early age have access to a constant display of nudity and heavy sexual interaction. Gone is the sort of information that once served as a marker on the way to adulthood.

Teen Years

Deprived of adequate parental authority, yet exposed at an early age to the adult world, today's teenager looks primarily to peers for identity and approval. As early as 1961 James Coleman observed that adolescents were cut off from adult society and looked to peers for guidelines to maturity. Hence, "society has within its midst a set of small teenage societies, which focus teenage interests and attitudes on things far removed from adult responsibilities, and which may develop standards that lead away from those goals established by the larger society."[17]

In the last thirty years, the image of teenagers has dramatically changed. Only a short time ago teens were portrayed as rather flighty, impulsive, given to rash schemes and overambitious projects, and in need of adult restraint, common sense, and good judgment. "In the media today the roles have been reversed, and we now have what has come to be known as the *adultified* child."[18]

According to TV critic Sally Bedell, the children in prime time today "tend to be miniature adults, possessing the tastes, mores, sensitivity, knowledge and even cynicism that until recent years were the exclusive province of maturity." These portrayals are not accidental, they are deliberate. Many scriptwriters and producers hold the mistaken idea that young people growing up in a frightening and unpredictable world need what the media experts call "realism."[19]

Contemporary American society, Elkind argues, has struck teenagers a double blow. "It has rendered them more vulnerable to stress while at the same time it has exposed them to more powerful stressful experiences than those faced by any previous generations of adolescents."[20]

The formula for big trouble is obvious to all but the blind. Start with substance abuse. It is now the leading cause of death among teenagers and accounts for more than ten thousand deaths every year. One recent survey of junior high school students indicated that 65 percent of the thirteen-year-olds had used alcohol at least once that year, some 35 percent used it once a month, and 20 percent used it once a week. The National Institute on Alcohol Abuse and Alcoholism reports that no less than 1.3 million teenagers between the ages of twelve and seventeen have serious drinking problems.[21]

Add to alcohol and drugs the widespread sexual activity among teens. At least among teenage girls, sexual encounters have more than tripled over the last two decades. "In contrast to the 1960s, when only 10 percent of teenage girls were sexually active, more than 50 percent are active today. By the age of nineteen at least 70 percent of young women have had at least one sexual experience."[22]

Finally, add the soaring suicide rates for teenagers, one of the leading causes of their deaths. "Five thousand teenagers commit suicide each year, and for each of these suicides fifty to one hundred youngsters make an unsuccessful attempt."[23]

Among the obvious victims of the radical shifts in the values Americans have come to treasure are today's teenagers. In order to reach emotional and social maturity teenagers need a clearly defined value system to push against while they test other values and discover their own. When the important adults in their lives do not know what their own values are—are not sure what is right and wrong, what is good and bad—the teenagers' task is extremely difficult.[24]

Resistance to Aging

The final arena of conflict between biblical religion and American culture in today's family is the attitude toward aging. Our society finds little use for the elderly. It is a society marked by the admiration of youth, beauty, celebrities, and style, so age holds a special terror and no little disdain. Even when seniors represent an increasing percentage of the American population, there is nothing less than a campaign against old age in American culture.

In his *Growing Old in America* David Hackett Fischer writes, "In the end, the discovery that one is old is inescapable. But most Americans are not prepared to make it." From his vantage point in Boston, Fischer describes men and women "on the far side of fifty" who try desperately to cling to the styles of youth. "Every twist and turn of teenage fashion" revolutionizes their costumes. But always, old is out and young is in.[25]

This dread of old age probably originates less in the stylish cult of youth than in the current cult of self. The fear of death takes on new intensity in a society that has turned its back on biblical religion and shows little interest in posterity.[26]

One of the traditional consolations of old age, shared by Christian believers in biblical times, is the belief that future generations will in some sense carry on our life's work. Our love and our work unite in a concern we feel for posterity, and specifically in our attempts to prepare the younger generation to carry on our tasks, including the dissemination of the gospel.

Our society no longer believes in the transmission of such accumulated wisdom or experience. In today's technological world change supposedly renders all knowledge obsolete and therefore nontransferrable. As a result most of us assume that grandparents have nothing to teach the younger generation. We expect our children to discover that their parents' ideas are old-fashioned and out-of-date. The central sorrow of old age in our society—often even more harrowing than frailty and loneliness—is the thought that all that we have lived for may go for naught.[27]

We are struck by the contrasting attitudes of the people of biblical times. The ancient Proverb says,

> Children's children are a crown
>   to the aged,
> and parents are the pride
>   of their children.[28]

Throughout its pages the Bible, like traditional American families, assumes that childhood is the pathway to maturity. But maturity, according to Christian teaching, is not going it alone or making something of oneself. Maturity is the most excellent way, the way of familial love. And parents and grandparents have a vital role to play in developing that maturity.

According to the apostle Paul, parents are responsible to bring their children up "in the training and instruction of the Lord."[29] In the Christian family the climate for this path to maturity is mutual respect "in Christ."

Judged according to this standard, American families today demand nothing less than a radical reordering of values. Surely Christians must be a significant part of that reordering. They can begin by clarifying their own thinking and passing on to their children the conviction that the life the gospel brings is a fundamental challenge to self-reliant individualism. Along with commitment to family unity, that new order involves personal sacrifices. Change in today's families will only come through a string of painful choices: living on less, listening to each other more, resisting appeals for "the latest," respecting age, spending more time together, reaching out to casualties of the American Dream, and perhaps most important, controlling the television.

Such a revolutionary lifestyle may be rare in today's American culture, but it is needed more than any of us can imagine. There is no substitute for it. The overthrow of selfish independence, like charity, begins at home.

FURTHER READING

David Elkind, *All Grown Up and No Place to Go: Teenagers in Crisis* (1984)
Joshua Meyrowitz, *No Sense of Place: The Impact of Electronic Media on Social Behavior* (1985)
Daniel Patrick Moynihan, *Family and Nation* (1987)
Neil Postman, *The Disappearance of Childhood* (1982)

Chapter 10, Notes

1. The quotation is found in *Connecticut Mutual Life Report on American Values in the '80s: The Impact of Belief* (Hartford, Conn.: Connecticut Mutual Life Insurance Co., 1981), 121.

2. See Judy Blume, *Superfudge* (New York: E. P. Dutton, 1980), 129, 136.

3. Robert N. Bellah and others, *Habits of the Heart* (New York: Harper & Row, 1985), 65.

4. Edward C. Stewart, *American Cultural Patterns: A Cross-Cultural Perspective* (LaGrange Park, Ill.: Intercultural, 1972), 32.

5. Bellah, *Habits of the Heart*, 65.

6. Beth Brophy, "Children under Stress," *U.S. News and World Report*, 27 October 1986, 58. See also Daniel Patrick Moynihan, *Family and Nation* (New York: Harcourt Brace Jovanovich, 1987), 46-48.

7. Lena Williams, "Teen-Age Sex: New Codes Amid the Old Anxiety," *New York Times*, National Section, 27 February 1989. Similar figures were reported earlier in C. Tietze, "Teenage Pregnancy: Looking Ahead to 1984," *Family Planning Perspectives* 10 (1978):205-7.

8. See David Elkind, *All Grown Up and No Place to Go: Teenagers in Crisis* (Reading, Mass.: Addison-Wesley Publishing Co., 1984), 130-35.

9. Ibid., 135.

10. See Christopher Lasch, *The Culture of Narcissism* (New York: Warner Books, 1979), 291-92.

11. Joshua Meyrowitz, *No Sense of Place: The Impact of Electronic Media on Social Behavior* (New York: Oxford University Press, 1985), 227, 229

12. Ibid., 229.

13. Elkind, *All Grown Up*, 109.

14. Meyrowitz, *No Sense of Place*, 242-43.

15. Elkind, *All Grown Up*, 100.

16. P. Charren and M. Sandler, *Changing Channels* (Reading, Mass.: Addison-Wesley Publishing Co., 1983), 63.

17. James Coleman, *The Adolescent Society* (New York: Free Press, 1961), 9.

18. Elkind, *All Grown Up*, 104.

19. "Junior Knows Best: TV's View of Children Today," *New York Times*, 19 September 1982.

20. Elkind, *All Grown Up*, 6.

21. Ibid., 6-7.

22. Ibid., 7.

23. Ibid. In the age group from fifteen to twenty-four, suicide is the third leading cause of death. Among persons of college age, it is the second leading cause. See Merton P. Strommen, *Five Cries of Youth* (New York: Harper & Row, 1988), 55.

24. Elkind, *All Grown Up*, 9.

25. Quoted in Lasch, *Culture of Narcissism*, 365-66.

26. Ibid., 354.

27. Ibid., 360.

28. Proverbs 17:6.

29. Ephesians 6:4.

Chapter Eleven
Love American Style

"Only the Americans have assumed that passion is destined to fulfillment."

—Arthur Schlesinger Jr.

*I*n the predawn darkness two days before Christmas, Nancy left her baby, only a few hours old, in a cardboard box by the door of the Clarksville post office. A short time later, a postal worker found the baby and carried her to Deaconess Hospital where she became an instant celebrity. But what the newspaper photos of smiling nurses hugging the blue-eyed bundle did not tell was the story of the anguish of a young, unwed mother from a religious home carrying the baby to term.

It is the story of an inexperienced girl caught up in a weekend affair with a man she hardly knew that ended with two terrified young women delivering a baby in the living room of their apartment, praying that the mother's labor cries would not alert the neighbors to their secret.

Nancy, as we are calling her, was already pregnant when she and her best friend moved to Wyoming from a southern city where they had attended junior college. She got pregnant after what she called a weekend fling with a truck driver she had met just a few weeks before. She was a virgin at the time, but, as she put it, "living proof that it only takes once." The man left town a few weeks later without ever learning he had fathered a child.

Coming from a religious family, Nancy was afraid to tell her father or stepmother about the pregnancy. "It would hurt them a lot," she said. "We are Southern Baptists and I don't think they would have understood." So she headed for Wyoming with her best girlfriend to hide the pregnancy and to make a fresh start in the West.

She never seriously considered abortion as a way out of her dilemma. "Life is too precious to abort it," she said. "It may be pure hell to go ahead with it and then have to give up the baby, but it is better than the alternative."

In Clarksville, the two young women found low-paying jobs. Nancy hid her condition by wearing loose-fitting clothes. She never saw a doctor or shared her secret with anyone except her girlfriend. Using only a library book on midwifery and a magazine article on childbirth, the girlfriend—who never before had witnessed a birth, let alone supervised one—delivered the baby the evening of December 22.

Holding the baby, Nancy realized she had to do something. So within hours she and her girlfriend waited in the car across from the post office until the postal worker arrived and found the box and the baby. The time was 5:45 A.M.

Just another story from the morning paper? Perhaps. I have changed the names and places, but it really did happen. And in our times, it is not all that unusual.

Americans have trouble dealing with love because they are not sure they know what it is. One of those observant Frenchmen, Raoul de Roussy de Sales, noted in 1938: "America appears to be the only country in the world where love is a national problem." In our Age of Therapy, interpersonal relations are an even deeper mystery.[1]

We all like to think of ourselves as informal and friendly people. And we do spend a lot of time in social activities. But our relationships are rarely deep and lasting because we avoid personal commitments. We don't like to get involved. We much prefer to pursue our social life under conditions that minimize our personal obligations. We can see this detachment in our personal friendships and in our romantic love.

Friendship without Commitments

With our passion for equality we Americans tend to relate to everyone in the same way. Our primary channel of communicating with others is a lighthearted informality. We rush to create first-name relationships. We often express the signs of friendship: the vigorous handshake, the ready smile, and the pat on the back.

We can find a cultural model for this informality in the traveling salesman and the airline attendant with the friendly smiles, the kidding, and the swapping of personal experiences, all within a two-hour flight to Chicago.

The meaning of *friend* is extremely vague. It stands for anyone from a passing acquaintance to a lifelong intimate. Our company of friends, however, usually centers around our activities, some shared experiences on the campus, in the neighborhood, or in the office. These realms of friendship seldom overlap. Office friends, for example, almost never meet neighborhood friends.

In all of these friendships lingers a reluctance to become deeply involved with other persons. Upon a closer look, American informality, which first appears to be a friendly, personal way of relating to others, is usually a form of depersonalization. The breeziness, humor, and kidding extend to everyone alike. Shunning discrimination, we try to keep everyone at a safe, depersonalized distance.[2]

This style of friendship can be traced in part to American self-reliant individualism. We like to "make our own way" and "stand on our own two feet." We want to be our "own person." When Alexis de Tocqueville visited the United States in 1831 he noticed this and remarked, "Democracy does not create strong attachments between man and man, but it does put their ordinary relations on an easier footing."

The contrast to other cultures is striking. Latins usually have strong attachments to their families and close friends. And among the Chinese, reliance on others is a desirable thing because dependence strengthens relationships. To be specific, Chinese parents take pride in their dependence upon their children and the support they receive from them.

Without the same strong family ties, Americans tend to relate to others as participants in some activity rather than as whole persons. Since most of us know the response we want to gain from others, we usually act in a way that will guarantee that response.

The most striking example of this is in the use of friendliness to make a sale. The telephone rings. We break off our conversation or interrupt our evening meal in order to hear some young man say, "Bruce, this is Al McGuire with Alco Improvements. How you doin'? Have you folks winterized your home with steel siding?" What disturbs us most in this sort of exchange is the light air of familiarity—the use of our first name and the assumed right to ask us about our personal life. That is American friendship in the service of sales.

The appeal of the phone call springs from the fact that Americans have an insatiable longing for the approval of others. Signs of friendship are a psychic necessity. If approval is not forthcoming, we are smitten with gnawing doubts about our acceptance and success. This makes it difficult for Americans to work under conditions that require some unpopular actions.[3]

The American style of social interaction, coupled with our cultural images of success and equality, encourages competition. Since each individual strives for his or her own personal goals, personal interactions often reveal some subtle forms of rivalry in the friendly joshing, freely given advice, quick repartee, or "friendly suggestion."

Tom, who has the last word, is one up on Charlie, at least until Charlie tells a better joke or gives a twist to the competition in some way that elevates him to the one-up position. Although this sort of behavior in interpersonal relations may seem innocent to Americans, such actions often appear as competition and subtle coercion to other peoples.[4]

In the New Testament, where the gospel's impact upon life is evident on every page, the ideal for human relations is no lighthearted friendship, it is what the Bible calls "sacrificial love." Such love begins with God. "God so loved the world that he gave his one and only Son, that whoever believes in him shall not perish but have eternal life."[5]

But it moves on to become the standard for all Christian relationships. "Be imitators of God," writes the apostle, "as dearly loved children and live a life of love, just as Christ loved us and gave himself up for us as a fragrant offering and sacrifice to God."[6]

Christians, then, living under the influence of America's dominant culture, can expect to encounter unusual resistance to the whole idea of commitment based on sacrificial love. The apostle's ideal for Christian relationships is likely to sound like an unintelligible message from Mars:

> Love is patient, love is kind. It does not envy, it does not boast, it is not proud. It is not rude, it is not self-seeking, it is not easily

angered, it keeps no record of wrongs. Love does not delight in evil but rejoices with the truth. It always protects, always trusts, always hopes, always perseveres.[7]

Love without Commitment

The contrast between American culture and biblical ideals is most striking in the expressions of romantic love. Romantic love has always had an air of mystery about it. That helps to make it exciting. There is nothing particularly new about that. The passion, however, with which Americans pursue their dreams of personal happiness through romance can only be compared to the religious zeal of a cultist.

Popular vocalists sing about it incessantly: "Everybody needs love." And ten thousand listeners nod their heads and say to themselves, "It's true." Advertisers know the magic of the mere thought, so they create their bumper stickers and billboards with the familiar red hearts to make the sale.

We can see the same passion among today's teenagers. Most Americans know some girl in the family or in the neighborhood—someone like Nancy—who can't talk to her parents, who runs away from home, experiments with drugs, and becomes pregnant by some guy who doesn't want anything to do with her once he discovers she is carrying a baby. That is the passion for love!

Americans, however, are victims of conflicting longings. We want the excitement of a dream of love that exists in our fantasies, but we also long for the security that comes from commitment to "the right" man or woman.

Robert Bellah and his team discovered this conflict during their extended study of American life. "In some ways," Bellah writes, "love is the quintessential expression of individuality and freedom." But at the same time, it is supposed to offer intimacy, mutuality, and sharing. Americans, then, are "torn between love as an expression of spontaneous inner freedom, a deeply personal, but necessarily somewhat arbitrary, choice, and the image of love as a firmly planted, permanent commitment, embodying obligations that transcend the immediate feelings or wishes of the partners in a love relationship."[8]

Love as personal freedom or love as personal commitment—that is the choice. Libertarians are on the side of freedom; Christians are on the side of commitment. The contrast is worth pursuing, for love as personal freedom and love as commitment differ in three important respects: its source, its meaning, and its promise.

The Source of Love

While Christians trace love to the life of God himself, the American romantic Dream (love as personal freedom) never explains where love comes from. The Dream never takes God into account. Love comes out of nowhere—without warning or preparation—and simply zaps you.

The romantic Dream we call love is something like measles. If we get caught in an infectious draft, we may wake up the next morning and discover that we caught it. No one can tell us where this romantic love comes from. We either catch it or we don't. As a result there is little we can do to prepare for it. We have no need for classes, seminars, or parental guidance. This love just happens.

Christian love has its mysteries, but the Bible is clear about one thing: Love comes from God. He is the source of a Christian's new life. He enters a believer's world and introduces a new set of values and affections. God's love brings a whole new reason to live.[9]

A picture of love American style appeared some years ago when the phones at the Seattle *Post Intelligencer* began ringing frantically. Some pilot had just written in smoke across the sky, "I love you," and dozens of lonely ladies wondered if they had a secret lover. It turned out to be Art Bell, a pilot who had finished a skywriting job elsewhere and had a bit of smoke left over. "I don't know why I did it," said Bell. "It just felt good."

The love the Bible recommends leaves us in no such suspense. At the outskirts of a near eastern city two thousand years ago, God planted a cross and said to all the world, "I love you."

Throughout its pages the Bible reminds us of God's yearning to rescue us from self-love and to change us. We discover that God is like a vinedresser caring for tender plants. He is like a shepherd watching after his sheep so prone to wander into danger and death. God, we read, is like a father yearning for his rebellious children to come to their senses and return home.

But the most striking image of God's love may be the picture we find in Hosea's prophecy. There we read that God is like a lover who experiences the agony of an adulterous wife. He suffers all the pain an earthly husband would feel—the anger, the thirst for revenge—yet he remains committed to his covenant promise. He forgives, he pursues, he restores his unfaithful bride. That is what God's love is like.

The Meaning of Love

From love's source, the Bible moves on to speak of love's meaning. "This is how God showed his love among us," we read. "He sent his one and only Son into the world that we might live through him. This is love: not that we loved God, but that he loved us and sent his Son as an atoning sacrifice for our sins."[10]

Love's meaning is the crux of the conflict between love in American culture and love in the gospel. When an American says, "I love you," what does he mean? Love, we know, "is a many-splendored thing." In tennis love means nothing; in marriage love means everything. And in between it can mean anything.

Consider three common examples from our daily conversations. We might say, "I love Dutch apple pie," or "I love red Japanese sports cars," or "I love pro football." But there is no way we can have the same emotion toward eating, driving, and watching television.

Loving Dutch apple pie means I want to eat it. I want to devour it. To be honest, I want to feel good—as it ceases to exist. That isn't love; that is exploitation.

Loving a sports car means I want to own one. I want to drive it, to feel the surge of power and turn a few heads. That isn't love; that is possession.

Loving pro football means I like to watch it. I enjoy getting the thrills without the bruises. But that isn't love, either; that is gratification.

In American culture, then, when some lover says "I love you," it is essential to figure out what he means. Does he want to devour you, possess you, enjoy you? This abuse of language helps to explain why Americans so often distort the relation between love and sex.

Christopher Lasch argues that the traditional bonds that once joined sex to love, marriage, and procreation have been strained to the breaking point by convenient contraceptives, legalized abortions, and a professed healthy acceptance of the body. Men and women in today's America pursue sexual pleasure as an end in itself, "unmediated even by the conventional trappings of romance." When emotional attachments get in the way of personal pleasure, both men and women try to achieve a strict separation between sex and feelings of attachment. The most prevalent form of this escape from emotional involvement is promiscuity, which masquerades as liberation. Men and women manipulate the emotions of others while protecting themselves against emotional injury. The result is a protective shallowness or cynical detachment in love and sex.[11]

The whole game, however, usually ends in frustration and anger because emotional intensity unavoidably clings to sex. The apostle Paul saw this clearly when he asked, "Do you not know that he who unites himself with a prostitute is one with her in body?"[12]

Christian love encourages the emotional attachments that surround sex and love because God's plan is to bring the two together in the commitment called marriage. Ideal Christian love is not expressed by love as passion (*eros*) alone, but by *agape*, love as commitment. This love is traceable to none other than God himself, who "loved us and sent his Son as an atoning sacrifice for our sins." This self-giving love is not primarily a feeling at all. It is an action we voluntarily take out of concern for another person. It is not an emotion we feel so much as a commitment we willingly make. *Agape* is gift and commitment and sacrifice rolled into one attitude we might call "care." That is the glimpse of love the gospel brings.

When this *agape* love does its work, our *eros* toward attractive people will be tempered by a concern for the welfare of people who are not attractive. And our demands for what we have coming to us will be blended with a desire that others get what they have coming too.

Of course, this power of *agape* will always work within the limits of our human weaknesses. If we think of Christian love only as a heavy obligation, we will be crushed under the weight of it. None of us is ever so free of self-concern as to think only of others' interests. That is an impossible dream! But the gospel does teach us that we can face the obligations of love out of the experience of love as God's gift.

The Promise of Love

Recent American culture knows little about that kind of love. It knows about pleasures. It knows little about responsibilities.

In their description of American culture, Bellah and his associates stress that a therapeutic view of love, so pervasive in American life, requires a "kind of selfishness." The popular what's-in-it-for-me kind of love denies all forms of obligation and commitment in relationships, replacing them only with the ideal of full, open, honest communication between two "self-actualized individuals."

Therapy is supposed to liberate people so that they get in touch with their wants and interests. The goal is self-realization, individuals free from "the artificial constraints of social roles, the guilt-inducing demands of parents and other authorities." For these "authentic" individuals, love means the free exchange of feelings, not enduring commitments resting on binding obligations.[13]

Americans like to think that today's love is free. It blows in the wind. It knows no ties. A lover is always "gentle on my mind." And if we don't like the way she looks or talks, we can always cut out.

That is what hosts of teens and singles and aging parents think love is. It is sex and pleasure without obligations. We hear the message in a thousand scripts and ten thousand love songs. Pastors confront it in scores of shattered families. In therapeutic American culture, love is an irresistible power. And if it hits you from across a sidewalk cafe or in a crowded lobby, give up everything for it. Follow love to the ends of the earth. Give up your family, your job, your friends. You must, because love makes you defenseless, vulnerable, irresponsible.

The trouble is, this cult of intimacy conceals a growing despair of finding it. Personal relations crumble under the weight they are called to bear. "It is clear, for example, that the growing incidence of divorce, together with the ever-present possibility that any given marriage will end in collapse, adds to the instability of family life and deprives the child of a measure of emotional security."[14]

Christian love is sharply different. The love the gospel brings is responsible; it assumes obligations; it is loyal; it hangs tough. "Dear friends," the apostle John writes, "since God so loved us, we also ought to love one another."[15]

Christian love finds no conflict in giving oneself to another and making promises to love, honor, and provide. Christians hold such a view of love because they know it isn't all magic feelings and "authentic" communication. They bear the name of the One who first loved them, and he made commitments. He kept his promise.

Ordinarily we wouldn't expect to find a reminder of love on a battlefield, but some unknown GI during the Vietnam War found a touch of beauty scrawled on a bombed-out wall. A bit of graffiti looked wistfully to the future and observed, "If the power of love could overcome the love of power, there would be no more war."

That holds true not only for nations; it is also a prescription for marriage. The Bible indicates that the transforming power of love is more than a faint hope. Life does not have to remain the same. Love as commitment can make a difference in our romance, our homes, our children, and our world. Christians should believe this for one supreme reason: it is the sort of love the Bible says begins with God himself.

FURTHER READING

Christopher Lasch, *The Culture of Narcissism* (1979)
Edward C. Stewart, *American Cultural Patterns: A Cross-Cultural Perspective* (1972)
Merton P. Strommen, *Five Cries of Youth* (1988)

Chapter 11, Notes

1. Quoted in Arthur Schlesinger, Jr., "An Informal History of Love U.S.A." in *Saturday Evening Post*, 31 December 1966, 37.
2. Edward C. Stewart, *American Cultural Patterns: A Cross-Cultural Perspective* (LaGrange Park, Ill.: Intercultural, 1972), 53-54.
3. Ibid., 58.
4. Ibid., 56.
5. John 3:16.
6. Ephesians 5:1-2.
7. 1 Corinthians 13:4-7.
8. Robert N. Bellah and others, *Habits of the Heart* (New York: Harper & Row, 1985), 93.

9. 1 John 4:8.

10. 1 John 4:9-10.

11. Christopher Lasch, *The Culture of Narcissism* (New York: Warner Books, 1979), 326-40.

12. 1 Corinthians 6:16.

13. Bellah, *Habits of the Heart*, 98-102.

14. Lasch, *Culture of Narcissism*, 320-21.

15. 1 John 4:11.

PART 4

NEW DREAMS

Now that we've gained some understanding of the relation of the gospel to the American Dream, we need to investigate some possible ways Christians can face the future. If Christians are a minority tolerated by the shapers of American culture, what can they do to preserve and propagate the gospel? We offer here some observations and suggestions for Christian action in our families, churches, and public life.

Chapter Twelve

Converting the Barbarians

"Modern secular liberalism has by now revealed the moral shallowness at its core. . . . Beneath official pieties, the Right embodies a wholly understandable yearning for an authentic, unchanging bedrock of moral values and beliefs that can withstand the disintegrative effects of modernization."

—T. J. Jackson Lears
in *No Place of Grace*

A fter Senator Robert Kennedy's death on June 6, 1968, hundreds of thousands of Americans waited outside St. Patrick's Cathedral in New York City to pay their last respects. Later in the week millions more, by means of television, watched the funeral train wend its way to Washington. Strains of "The Battle Hymn of the Republic" provided the musical background of the somber scenes. The funeral on Saturday vested the slain leader with additional sacred symbols of the nation's destiny. The service was in part religious, in part secular.

On the one hand, a Roman Catholic funeral mass

offered to the grieving the comfort of the Catholic doctrines of hope, resurrection, and heavenly reward for a life well lived. The funeral liturgy affirmed in the face of death: "For those who have been faithful all the way, life is not ended but merely changed. And when this earthly abode dissolves, an eternal dwelling place awaits them in Heaven."

On the other hand, the funeral echoed the ideals of secular America. Senator Edward Kennedy, quoting from and commenting on a speech by his brother, offered the secular affirmation:

> "Our future may lie beyond our vision, but it is not completely beyond our control. It is the shaping impulse of America that neither faith nor nature nor the irresistible tides of history, but the work of our own hands, matched to reason and principle, will determine our destiny. There is pride in that, even arrogance, but there is also experience and truth. In any event, it is the only way we can live."
> This is the way he lived.[1]

This powerful national event epitomizes the cultural context in which American Christians worship, witness, and serve today. The last three decades have seen the biblical and the secular dreams for America drift farther and farther apart. Americans no longer share the same code of ethics, the same religious faith, the same idea of patriotism, or the same images of the Great Society.

To America's academic, judicial, and media elite, these recent decades have brought great advances in human freedom and dignity: the easing of divorce laws, the tolerance of new life-styles, the legalization of abortion, and the end of artistic censorship. To conservative Americans, including hosts of Christians, the same decades are marked by moral decadence, national decline, and a social revolution comparable to the barbarian overthrow of the Christian Roman Empire.

Recent events have left many Christians crying out for reform. But where does reform begin? Some believers are so angry over abortions on demand and prejudice against Christians in public school classrooms that they are calling for nothing less than a "reconstruction" of the American republic on the explicit laws of God. They challenge the whole enlightened, progressive creed of liberalism.

Many have used their bodies as barricades before the doorways of abortion clinics. Others have marched in the streets for Right to Life causes or worked tirelessly for the recall of some school board member or superintendent. Driven by their frustrations, Christians by the thousands are seeking access to power in American public life.

Unfortunately for these zealous believers, power in America is limited and diffused. The republic was created that way and massive immigrations to metropolitan areas have made pluralism a fact of life. Consensus under the Puritan vision of a moral America is a distant memory. The values of the secular tradition, especially the exclusion of churches from seats of power, have been welcomed by too many for too long. The Puritan myth, emphasizing God's plan for America, has been replaced by a much fuzzier image of restless minorities competing for a place in the American sun.

Does that mean the Christian mission to America has been rescinded? Must Christians settle for winning individual souls here and there? Not at all. Christians are a vital part of America's future. Evangelism remains a mandate. The preservation of the traditional family, the multiplication of spiritually vibrant congregations, the Christian education of the young and newly converted, and Christian ministries of compassion in the public realm remain priorities for Christians in America. Only now, in the presence of the secular barbarians, these ministries must be conducted as strategies of a minority, not the party of power.

The Christian Mind

What American Christians must do, then, is to return to the biblical gospel with a deeper understanding and a renewed commitment. It must be the controlling theme of the church's assembled worship and teaching and the motivation for its Christian care for a broken world.

For a half-century or more twentieth-century secular evangelists have been disseminating another gospel, which is not really good news at all. Harry Blamires has called it, appropriately, "The Myth of Escalating Emancipation."

This new myth claims that every step forward in the intellectual, social, and political fields is a part of a movement in universal liberation. Minorities are being liberated from political oppressors, labor from slavery to capitalists, women from servitude to men, children from the tyranny of parents, citizens from the constraints of poverty, homosexuals from the laws against perversion, couples from the prison of lifelong marriage, renters from restrictive housing codes, and monkeys from ruthless researchers. The myth stresses an "escalating emancipation" because life seems to have no end of tyrants and limitations. The business of dismantling past restrictions must go on indefinitely.

That some of these liberations are highly desirable has encouraged the notion that all of them must be. This barbarian myth, then, calls for faith in the certainty of human progress in overcoming all restrictions.

This secular gospel, however, is a Christian heresy. It rests on the assumption that mankind has progressed, not by the discipline of the ego, but by feeding its insatiable appetite. The fact that many devotees of the gospel of self-liberation end up enslaved to some chemical, sexual, or emotional addiction seems to make no impression on its zealous evangelists.[2]

Some years ago the Norwegian dramatist Ibsen

told the story of Peter Gynt going to a mental hospital and surprisingly finding that no one in the place seemed crazy. They all talked so sensibly and discussed their plans with such precision and concern that he felt sure they must be sane. Mystified, Gynt asked the doctor about his discovery.

"They're mad," said the doctor. "They talk very sensibly, I admit, but it is all about themselves. They are, in fact, most intelligently obsessed with self. It's self—morning, noon, and night. We can't get away from self here. We lug it along with us, even through our dreams. O yes, young sir, we talk sensibly, but we're mad right enough."[3]

Life under the sway of the secular gospel may well be compared to that mental institution. Adherents to the Myth of the Escalating Emancipation are obsessed with self. They talk incessantly about their feelings, their rights, their money, their toys, their sex.

In that restricted little world the gospel of the Lord Jesus Christ is nothing less than a liberating announcement from the sane world beyond the walls of the hospital. It tells us about a life vastly different from the life of getting and grabbing, the cramped world of appetites and impulses. It speaks of willing surrender and the rewards of discipline in the expansive world of the life of God.

Biblical sanity recognizes a liberating world beyond this life of sex, spending, and entertainment. Secular thinking in America persistently treats this world as The Thing. The Christian, however, believes that human life and human history are in the hands of God. The whole universe is sustained by the Almighty's power and love. The natural order is dependent upon that supernatural Order; time is contained within eternity. This earthly life is a temporary place, a significant preparation for another, final world beyond the grave.

Biblical sanity holds that human life is handicapped by a pervasive evil in society and in the human heart, every human heart. Secular Americans assume that human nature is basically good and that life can operate reasonably well without religious and moral judgments. Christians, however, have, as Blamires puts it, "an acute and sensitive awareness of the power and spread of evil upon the human scene."

The key sin in the Christian moral system is egocentric pride, that perversion of human thinking and choosing by which the self becomes the center of the universe. The key virtue in the Christian moral system is obedience, that commitment of self in thought and act by which God is revered as the center of the universe. The Christian goal, then, is to make all of life's activities and relationships a fit offering to God.

Biblical sanity attests to an objective standard of truth, the basis for a meaningful view of life and for morality in the world. Contemporary Americans reflect the secular habit of asserting the opinionated self as the only judge of truth. For the secular mind, broadcast daily in hosts of talk radio programs, religious convictions are a matter of individual preference related not to objective truth but to personal need or taste. Christianity, however, recognizes divine revelation as the touchstone of truth. Its sanity starts with the hard, factual quality of truth, a series of special events surrounding the life and death of Jesus Christ in first-century Palestine.

Finally, *biblical sanity highlights the concern for people.* One of the prominent marks of contemporary life is the reverence for technology, the daily use of the maximum number of gadgets. The good life is often equated with how many new products one possesses. In Christianity, however, what counts is not products but people. This Christian sense of the sacredness of human personality is grounded in the fact that God became man.

Every human being, regardless of class or condition, is more than a consumer or a statistic. He or she is the center of God's intentional love.[4]

What is the significance of all this for America's

future? For over a generation now public life in America has been centrifugal. Recent therapeutic culture has taught us to expect from government our personal rights, benefits, and entitlements. We have stumbled along in pursuit of freedom without a moral center of gravity offering any restraining force or basis for life in communities. As a result, almost any social behavior could lay claim to legitimacy. If we want to preserve the American experience, public life in the future must be more centripetal. We need to move away from the individual toward community concerns. And that is where the gospel comes in.[5]

When the good news about God's love enters the human heart, it begins to alter our attitudes from a "what-do-I-get-out-of-it" attitude to one of "what-can-I-give-to-others." In this sense the gospel really does "convert" us. Life is no longer what can I expect from my marriage, my church, and my government, but what can these "civil" communities expect from me. Thus one of the basic needs in American public life today, the shift in public expectations, is addressed by the Christian gospel.

In the uncertain days ahead, civility and community call Christians to a clear understanding of the gospel and the behavioral consequences of life under the grace of God. Need alone demands that Christians in their personal lives, their homes, and their churches probe, teach, and share the gospel of the Lord Jesus Christ. Who else will bring some semblance of sanity to the Myth of Escalating Emancipations?

The Christian Family

The restoration of community begins in American families. The future demands that Christian couples take their vows before God with greater dedication and resist the pressures of the media, the secular distortions of love, and the ease of divorce.

The home is the place for learning those elementary lessons essential to any humane society, such as respect for authority, the sanctity of life, and the keeping of promises. Christians who valiantly attempt to preserve family values from the rapacious barbarians are among the American minority maintaining this function of civil society. In American life today the simple practice of teaching our children to thank God for their daily food is a telling blow struck against secularism.

At the conclusion of his exposé called *The Disappearance of Childhood*, Neil Postman asks, Is the individual powerless to resist what is happening in American society? The answer is no. But resistance of contemporary styles will likely be interpreted as an act of rebellion against American culture. For husbands and wives to remain married is itself an act of disobedience and "an insult to the spirit of a throwaway culture." It is also at least "ninety percent un-American" to remain close to one's extended family so that children can experience the meaning of kinship and the values of deference and responsibility to elders.

In the same way, to insist that one's children learn the discipline of delayed gratification, or modesty in their sexuality, or self-restraint in manners, language, and style is to assume a position in opposition to almost every social trend. And the most rebellious act of all may be the attempt to control the media's access to one's children.

Some parents are committed to doing all of these things, defying the directives of the barbarians. But these parents, says Postman, are not only helping their children to have a childhood; they are, at the same time, creating an intellectual elite. In the short run children who grow up in such homes will, as adults, be favored by business, the professions, and the media themselves. And in the long run, parents who resist the spirit of the age, says Postman, will contribute to the Monastery Effect. Like the Benedictines of the earlier dark ages, they will help to keep alive a humane tradition.

"It is not conceivable," Postman writes, "that our culture will forget that it needs children. But it is halfway toward forgetting that children need childhood. Those who insist on remembering shall perform a noble service." Christians must remember and be courageous in their defense of traditional family values: worship, unity, respect, generosity, sobriety, modesty, and love.[6]

The Church in America

In the doctrine of the church, Christians preserve another resource for a "kinder and gentler" America. As God designed it the church is to be in the world but not wholly of it. The trick, then, is for Christians to work on two fronts simultaneously: in "outreach" to the wider community and in "uplift" of their own "common life in Christ." In brief, churches need to move into the open spaces in public life and to enlist deeper commitment from Christian believers.

To understand what this means in America today, we need to consider the common image of the larger society. Christians, like many other Americans, look upon their society as fragmented, disconnected, often cold and competitive, sometimes violent. Individual mobility and urban sprawl have shattered neighborhood ties, and corporate bureaucracies have depersonalized relations in the workplace. The family is in trouble, with parents forced to spend more time earning a living than raising children. Divorce, suicide, crime, alcoholism—all the signs of personal and social disorder—are on the rise. And periodically the economy seems completely out of control.

This image may be stark and overdrawn, but it is the one that motivates many churches in their attempts to "create Christian community." They think of Christian fellowship in sharp contrast to mass society. Instead of conflict, they want comfort. Instead of distance between persons, they want intimacy. Instead of criticism, they want affirmation and good will.[7]

This "fellowship" is helpful, no doubt, to some, but it is inadequate if it is merely a haven from the storms of life outside. The church's potential for cultural renewal lies in the fact that it is both in the world and not wholly of it. That is basic to the infusion of Christian values in our democratic society.

On the one hand, the church is vital for America's future only as it sees its calling as detached from the established social order. "My kingdom," said Jesus, "is not of this world." The church's primary call is to prepare people for the life to come. If Christians do not make worship, prayer, and religious education important, who will?

On the other hand, the church is in the world in that it serves both as a critic of all fashionable public and private immoralities and as a sponsor of decency, civility, and justice. "In the world" also means the church must resist all those pressures in a secular society that try to restrict religion to the private life. In the midst of moral darkness, what good is a candle under a bushel?

The "new community" in the days ahead must maintain this distinctive calling. The church in the twenty-first century must distinguish a meaningful Christian engagement of American culture in its outreach ministry and a distinctive Christian alternative to American culture in its worshiping community. It must break through the walls of isolation from American public life by the use of methods and ministries that make sense to secular-minded Americans. But at the same time, the church must resist assimilation by that same American culture by maintaining a distinctively Christian worship, message, discipline, and life-style.[8]

The calling is an old one: loving the sinner but not his sin. It is counseling and comforting the divorced, while calling the church to lifelong marriages. It is reaching out to latchkey kids, while encouraging the establishment of united Christian homes. It is caring for unwed victims of sexual freedom, while calling pornography what it is, a crime against decency.

Assimilation by and isolation from the surrounding culture are constant threats to Christianity in a democracy. During the last half-century American Christians have struggled with both dangers and have proved only partially successful in their attempts to infuse American culture with biblical values.[9]

Recent Christian attempts to respond to American society make one thing clear. The most important service churches can offer to American public life is the recovery of the benefits of duty, discipline, and God's law. What can rights mean without responsibilities? What can forgiveness mean without sin? What can morality in government or on Wall Street mean if we can't identify a crime?

The churches' return to the meaning and place of moral values in private and public life may be their greatest contribution to a humane capitalism and a civil democracy. Through all possible means "the old-fashioned" gospel must be presented as the foundation of a disciplined, caring, and humane life-style.

Christians in Public Life

Finally, what can Christians do to enter and reshape American public life itself? This is the toughest question of all. In the past Christians have proved strikingly creative in reaching out; we can hope they will prove equally creative in the future. I mention here three possibilities: political activity, "life-style enclaves," and "little platoons."

As public life in America has become narrowly identified with politics and government, increasing numbers of conservative Christians have moved vigorously into various political and legal battles (abortion, prayer in public schools, violence on television). Their intent is simple, their goal is clear: to exercise political and cultural power—to use the courts and the ballot—to restore traditional morality to their communities.

In a pluralistic society such a mission is filled with obvious political risks and with the very real spiritual dangers of intolerance and arrogance. Where is the line between religious and political activity? How will the American public distinguish moral principle from partisan politics?[10]

Up to a point, Christian participation in the formation of public policy, particularly on issues with clear moral content, strengthens their ability to fulfill their God-given purpose. If the churches were to remain silent on civil rights or abortion, they would soon lose moral credibility.

But if Christians become too involved in the push-and-shove routine of politics, they will eventually appear to the general public as special pleaders for ideological causes, one more political faction. Each church will have to decide for itself where this point of political and moral peril comes. But it is in their own, as well as the public's, interest that Christians be thoughtful and prudent in pushing the limits of public tolerance.[11]

Christians need to temper their enthusiasm for politics by recognizing that public life is much broader than politics. Public life is basically our life among strangers, with whom we are interdependent whether we like it or not. Though we are strangers to one another, we occupy common space, share common resources, and have common opportunities. If Christians hope to reach out to others in this wider sphere, most will need a refresher course in ways to communicate with strangers.

In recent years public life has shriveled as we live and work in those spaces where the public cannot intrude. We sleep, arise, and eat in the privacy of our own homes. We drive to our jobs in the privacy of an automobile. We park in an underground garage and work in a space where only colleagues are allowed. After work, we head back to our cars and back to our homes with little chance for interaction with strangers.

In our free time, when we might mingle with the

public in a park or at a sporting event, we are more inclined to watch the parade or game on TV in the privacy of our living rooms. As our public experience dwindles, we lose our sense of comfort and at-homeness in the world. Lacking a culture of local community, we turn to the culture conveyed by the mass media and the mass market.[12]

If Christians entertain any hope of shaping American public life, they will need to break through the walls that isolate them from strangers. Robert Bellah and his colleagues have noted that in our metropolitan areas, where hostile groups often collide, our demands of work, family, and community are sharply separated and often contradictory.

As a result we have created substitutes for traditional public events in small-town America in what we may call "life-style enclaves." These suburban expressions of our private lives are "communities" we enter by personal choices, usually linked with our leisure and consumption. They range from memberships at the country club to square dance gatherings, from rose garden clubs to craft fairs. Most are based upon individual choices that free us from traditional ethnic and religious boundaries. The advantage of these "enclaves" in suburban America lies in the opportunities they afford us to retreat from the utilitarian world of work into an expressive world of friendly community.[13]

The danger for churches lies in the possibility of it being accepted by the public as just another "life-style enclave," a weekend activity for the religiously inclined. There is, however, a more positive possibility. Since these enclaves are basic to social relationships in contemporary American culture, what are the avenues of access to these "communities" for some gospel witness? How can we build bridges of friendship from these communities to The Christian Community?

Finally, the possibilities of Christians sending out "little platoons" among the barbarians was underscored recently by Charles Colson. The expression "little platoons" apparently came first from British statesman Edmund Burke. Colson, however, uses it to designate voluntary groups of Christians serving others in works of mercy or forming alliances with others to oppose injustices in American society. These individuals and groups, says Colson, are the "salt and light" that Jesus mentioned.

Despite all the ballyhoo, Colson writes, feeding the hungry did not originate with mass rallies by rock stars. "Christians have been doing it since the church began, not for T-shirts and pop albums, but in obedience to Christ's command to care for those in need. Organizations such as World Vision, Catholic Relief Services, the Salvation Army, and millions of local churches have for generations been feeding the hungry, housing the homeless, and clothing the needy without glamorous carrot-and-stick razzle-dazzle so recently discovered by the rich and famous."[14]

In the memory of Western peoples, the classic example of Christian ministry during the decline of civil and humane culture comes from the final days of the Roman Empire. For 620 years Rome had seen no foreign invader outside its walls. Then suddenly in 410 Alaric, the Visigoth leader, with his Arian hordes was besieging the city. Visigoths charged through the gates and plundered the city, temple by temple, palace by palace, leaving devastation and ruin in their path. The glory of the "queen of cities" was suddenly gone, forever. The fall of the Roman Empire!

Today social commentators often draw comparisons with our own American culture. When Rome fell, and morality and civility with it, St. Benedict—hardly aware of what he was doing—set about to construct new forms of community, his monastic houses, to sustain the spiritual life through the coming ages of barbarism. Today's barbarians, it is true, are not threatening the frontiers; they have been governing for some time. But what matters for us are the new forms of community within which civility and moral life can be sustained through the dark ages ahead of us.[15]

We know that the last forty years have not been without their social and cultural advances. Minorities enjoy unprecedented civil liberties today. Hundreds of technological developments—new drugs, organ transplants, laser treatments—have reduced human pain and prolonged life. Even some previously socially acceptable but damaging personal habits, such as cigarette smoking, have fallen under cultural criticism.

Still, when we assess the heart of our culture's character—the pleasure-seeking, opinionated self—the immediate need for new forms of community for intellectual, spiritual, and moral life is evident. That is the significance of ministries such as Charles Colson and his Prison Fellowship, Father Ritter and his Covenant House, and Martin Luther King, Jr. and his civil rights movement. They are symbols of the gospel's future in America.

The return to the biblical and republican traditions of American culture, once obvious in the nation's small towns, must come now in ways that speak to contemporary urban needs. These symbols from prison cells and city streets are both realistic and encouraging—realistic because they reveal the dark side of the recent American Dream, and encouraging because they magnify the light of the Christian gospel.

As we approach the twenty-first century, then, America's 380,000 local churches can find both hope and challenge because the good news about God's kingdom, despite America's shifting culture, is still capable of penetrating the nation's prisons, streets, and legislatures, just as in earlier days it illumined the dense, barbarian forests of Europe.

FURTHER READING

Harry Blamires, *Where Do We Stand?* (1980)
Charles Colson, *Kingdoms in Conflict* (1987)
Parker J. Palmer, *The Company of Strangers* (1981)

Chapter 12, Notes

1. See Conrad Cherry, ed., *God's New Israel: Religious Interpretations of American Destiny* (Englewood Cliffs, N.J.: Prentice-Hall, 1971), 4-6.

2. See Harry Blamires, *Recovering the Christian Mind* (Downers Grove, Ill.: InterVarsity Press, 1988), 110-12.

3. Quoted in W. E. Sangster, *The Pure in Heart* (Nashville: Abingdon Press, n.d.), 232.

4. For these four points of Christian thinking, see Harry Blamires, *The Christian Mind* (Ann Arbor, Mich.: Servant Books, 1978).

5. See Lance Morrow's "To Revive Responsibility," *Time*, 23 February 1981, 73.

6. Neil Postman, *The Disappearance of Childhood* (New York: Delacorte Press, 1979), 152-53.

7. See Parker J. Palmer, *The Company of Strangers* (New York: Crossroad, 1981), 118-19.

8. I can think of two influential evangelical churches that are pioneering in ministering to secular-minded Americans: Bear Valley Baptist Church in Denver and Willow Creek Community Church in suburban Chicago. See Frank Tillapaugh's *Unleashing the Church* (Ventura, Calif.: Regal Books, 1982) and Bill Hybels, "Speaking to the Secular Mind," *Leadership* 9 (Summer 1988):28-34.

9. During the 1960s and 1970s, the so-called mainline churches were socially and politically active in efforts to influence national policies on such issues as race, poverty, housing, public education, and urban renewal. In the 1980s the center stage of partisan politics shifted to evangelicals, fundamentalists, and charismatics, who tried to shape national and local policies on prayer in the public schools, abortion, restrictions on homosexuality, women's rights, aid to nonpublic schools, and pornography. Results on both sides of the liberal-conservative line were hotly debated.

Today we can applaud the mainline denominations for their share in the social victories of the civil rights movement. Too many mainline Christians, however, during the 1960s and 1970s got the extraordinary idea that if they gave themselves to the solution of social problems in lieu of religious observances, then grateful secular people would be mystically infected with some vague spirituality. Supposedly, they would see God's hand at work in America. But it didn't happen.

At the same time, conservative Protestants in more recent years worked out their own compromises with America's therapeutic culture. A review of popular evangelical literature reveals a preoccupation with narcissistic themes of happiness, self, and joy. The traditional note of self-denial in evangelical ethics has often been displaced by themes of self-fulfillment. See James Davison Hunter, *American Evangelicalism* (New Brunswick, N.J.: Rutgers University Press, 1983), 97-99.

10. A study by the Times Mirror Corporation in 1988 titled "The People, Press and Politics" revealed that white evangelical Protestants, white non-evangelical Protestants and white Catholics are more Republican than their parents. Among white evangelical Protestants, those who identify themselves as "born-again" Christians, 47 percent said their parents were Democrats and 27 percent said their parents were Republicans. Today, however, 35 percent identified themselves as Republicans and 29 percent as Democrats. Among white non-evangelical Protestants and white Catholics the shift was not as strong.

11. For this sensible assessment I am indebted to A. James Reichley's *Religion in American Public Life* (Washington, D.C.: The Brookings Institution, 1985), 359.

12. See Palmer, *Company of Strangers*, 21, 81.

13. Robert N. Bellah, *Habits of the Heart* (New York: Harper & Row, 1985), 180.

14. Charles Colson, *Kingdoms in Conflict* (Grand Rapids: Zondervan Publishing House, 1987), 254.

15. See Alasdair MacIntyre, *After Virtue: A Study in Moral Theory* (Notre Dame, Ind.: University of Notre Dame Press, 1981), 244-45.

For Further Reading

Bell, Daniel. *The Cultural Contradictions of Capitalism*. New York: Basic Books, 1976.

Bellah, Robert N., and others. *Habits of the Heart*. New York: Harper & Row Publishers, 1985.

Bercovitch, Sacvan. *The American Jeremiad*. Madison, Wisc.: University of Wisconsin Press, 1978.

Blamires, Harry. *Where Do We Stand?* Ann Arbor, Mich.: Servant Books, 1980.

Colson, Charles. *Kingdoms in Conflict*. Grand Rapids: Zondervan Publishing House, 1987.

Dayton, Edward R. *Whatever Happened to Commitment?* Grand Rapids: Zondervan Publishing House, 1984.

Guinness, Os. *The Gravedigger File*. Downers Grove, Ill.: InterVarsity Press, 1983.

Lasch, Christopher. *The Culture of Narcissism*. New York: Warner Books, 1979.

Lears, T. J. Jackson. *No Place of Grace: Antimodernism and the Transformation of American Culture 1880-1920*. New York: Pantheon Books, 1981.

Linder, Robert D., and Richard V. Pierard. *Twilight of the Saints: Biblical Christianity and Civil Religion in America*. Downers Grove, Ill.: InterVarsity Press, 1978.

Marsden, George, ed. *Evangelicalism and Modern America*. Grand Rapids: Wm. B. Eerdmans Publishing Co., 1984.

Mead, Sidney E. *The Nation with a Soul of a Church*. New York: Harper & Row Publishers, 1975.

Meyrowitz, Joshua. *No Sense of Place: The Impact of Electronic Media on Social Behavior*. New York: Oxford University Press, 1985.

Mooney, Christopher F. *Public Virtue*. Notre Dame, Ind.: University of Notre Dame Press, 1986.

Moorhead, J. H. "Theological Interpretations and Critiques of American Society and Culture." *Encyclopedia of the American Religious Experience*. Edited by C. H. Lippy and P. W. Williams. New York: Charles Scribner's Sons, 1988.

Neuhaus, Richard John. *The Naked Public Square*. Grand Rapids: Wm. B. Eerdmans Publishing Co., 1984.

Newbigin, Lesslie. *Foolishness to the Greeks*. Grand Rapids: Wm. B. Eerdmans Publishing Co., 1986.

Noll, Mark A. *One Nation under God? Christian Faith and Political Action in America*. San Francisco: Harper & Row Publishers, 1988.

Postman, Neil. *Amusing Ourselves to Death*. New York: Viking Press, 1985.

_____. *The Disappearance of Childhood*. New York: Delacorte Press, 1982.

Reichley, A. James. *Religion in American Public Life*. Washington, D.C.: The Brookings Institution, 1985.

Schaller, Lyle E. *It's a Different World*. Nashville: Abingdon Press, 1987.

Silk, Mark. *Spiritual Politics*. New York: Simon and Schuster, 1988.

Stewart, Edward C. *American Cultural Patterns: A Cross-Cultural Perspective*. LaGrange Park, Ill.: Inter-cultural, 1972.

Vitz, Paul C. *Psychology as Religion: The Cult of Self-Worship*. Grand Rapids: Wm. B. Eerdmans Publishing Co., 1977.

Wald, Kenneth D. *Religion and Politics in the United States*. New York: St. Martin's Press, 1987.

Woodbridge, John D., Mark A. Noll, and Nathan O. Hatch. *The Gospel in America*. Grand Rapids: Zondervan Publishing House, 1979.